The Trenchard Touch

Previous Publications

By the same Author

Under name of Jonathan Havard

Blood and Judgment
Heinemann and Pan

The Stockholm Syndrome
Heinemann and Pan

Coming of Age
Heinemann and Mandarin

The Price of Fame
Heinemann

Under name of Cyril Havard

Medical Eponyms
Barry Rose Law Publishers

THE TRENCHARD TOUCH

Cyril Havard

Countrywise Press
Chichester
West Sussex, England

© 2000 Cyril Havard and Countrywise Press

ISBN 1 902681 13 4

All rights reserved. No part of this publication may be reproduced, stored in a retrieval system, or transmitted, in any form or by any means, electronic, mechanical, photocopying, recording or otherwise, without prior written permission of the author and publishers.

Printed and bound by
The Cromwell Press, Trowbridge, Wiltshire

**Published by
Countrywise Press
East Row, Little London
Chichester
West Sussex, England**

Contents

Prologue	To Granny and to Jim	xi
Chapters 1-12	Hard Fact	1-151
Epilogue	Pure Fantasy	152
Bibliography		161
Index		171

Illustrations in this Volume

Prologue   -   Hindenberg

Chapter 1   -   de Havilland's First Aeroplane

Chapter 2   -   DH2

Chapter 3   -   Trenchard

Chapter 4   -   Richtofen

Chapter 5   -   DH4

Chapter 6   -   Amy Johnson

Chapter 7   -   Comet

Chapter 8   -   Aircrew

Chapter 9   -   Mosquito and Lancaster in Flight

Chapter 10 -   Harris

Chapter 11 -   Devastation

Chapter 12 -   Trenchard

Epilogue   -   Schloss

Prologue

My early childhood was spent in Aberystwyth on the coast of Cardigan Bay, a small town then given to fishing, farming, university life and various forms of worship. I still recall the salty tang of rope and canvas as the fishing smacks unloaded their catch, the sight, sounds and smells as flocks of sheep were driven to market along Llanbadarn Road by trudging monoglot Welshmen, afoot before dawn, pearl eyed collies slinking at their heels. Too young to appreciate the finer points of interfaculty feuds at the founder university college by the sea, so absorbing to my parents, I, as a member of Holy Trinity choir, was nevertheless old enough to be aware of the churchgoers' wary coexistence with those who frequented chapel, be it Shiloh or Tabernacle. An intensely academic town, a forum for strong emotions, it was dominated from on high, like some Celtic Acropolis, by the National Library of Wales, a legal deposit library to match the Bodleian, proudly wrested from the Welsh capital.

After six p.m. on a winter's day it was impossible to get in or out of the town by public transport but the town's outwardly sleepy, introverted atmosphere, particularly when spared the daily Anglo-Saxon invasion when "trippers" from West Bromwich and Kidderminster were out of season, belied the true intellectual nature of the place, intensified as it was during the winter months by its utter isolation. At such times, for those still to experience living in a house with electricity, the only evidence that a world existed out there, beyond Plynlimon Mountain, was a distant voice, waxing and waning amongst the crackles and oscillations of a battery driven wireless set. In the late twenties and early thirties, for a small boy whose mind ran along more practical lines, to find himself in such a town, obsessed as it was with law, theology, philosophy, music and botany, was to feel as remote from the world of mechanical progress and aeronautical adventure as it was possible to be. For this reason, one of my earliest childhood memories, possibly *the* earliest, is stark, still sharply outlined after almost seventy years.

We were sitting at breakfast, the kitchen door open on to a heavenly, cloudless summer morning. I must have been the first to hear the strange noise. I was certainly the first to react. I got down from the table and moved, drawn to the door as if in some mesmeric trance exerted by some supernatural force. There must have been some cause for concern about my appearance as my sudden, unexplained departure from the table did not provoke the maternal rebuke such ill manners would have normally excited.

Out into the garden, still sleep-walking, I looked upwards, open-mouthed. Only the sudden arrival overhead of an alien spacecraft would produce such speechless wonder in a young boy today. It came slowly, remorselessly out of the early morning sun, preceded by a crescendo of roaring power never dreamed of by a boy exposed previously only to the rattling grumble of the daily London bus passing the front door.

Gradually it took shape. First a sharp, pointed nose, then a rounded sinister length as it came beam on. Pictures pored over in that trusty Christmas present, *The Modern Boy Annual*, had not prepared me for the majestic enormity of its true being. The whining, whirring propellers threatened even more than the swish of Fatty Griffiths's, the schoolmaster's cane. There was a glint of glass from its underbelly as if its Cyclopean eye had picked me out for particular inspection. Was I to be plucked from the bosom of a loving family to be carried to some distant galaxy as an interesting specimen of primitive life on planet Earth? No; it was passing. For all its menace I wanted it to stay but it obviously had no interest in one small, awe struck boy. I almost expected a contemptuous wiggle of its rudder as it arrogantly presented its stern to me.

"The Hindenberg." My father's voice - with an edge to it.

I had not heard him, standing protectingly behind me. He said nothing more, turning on his heel, leaving me to watch regretfully the diminishing presence. Many years later, older and wiser, I wondered at my father's thoughts, seeing overhead, uninvited, unchallenged, the compatriots of someone who had put a bullet through his shoulder on the Somme, releasing him from sights and sounds that had turned a gentle, courageous man into a permanent anxiety state.

Sadly, I watched the airship disappear. From my vantage point, the limit of my visual world was the National Library. As the craft was blocked from my view by mundane bricks and mortar, it trailed its sound for a few further titillating minutes. It left the mind of a small boy who had never been out of Wales, struggling to imagine, if he were to draw a straight line from our garden through the National Library of Wales and beyond, what countries existed out there to the west, destined soon to feel that chill predatory shadow.

From that day, I have been unable to allow any aircraft to pass overhead without stretching my neck to watch it, wondering at its distant destination. It's less interesting now. At thirty thousand feet they all look the same; but they remain compelling. They all sound the same too - gone are the days when you could diagnose a Spitfire or a Dakota or a Blenheim or a Harvard trainer with your eyes closed. The best one can hope for now is the distinction between a jet and a turbo-prop or a helicopter. But the sound of an aero engine still demands attention.

The next invasion of Aberystwyth's air space was a much more friendly affair. Sir Alan Cobham's Air Circus came to town, turning a farmer's field, not a mile from my home, into a frenzy of roaring, whirring, coughing, spluttering excitement. The spectacle of high flying aerobatics provided a gracious backdrop to the raucous rough and tumble of low level daring as dastardly enemy spies were bombed with flour bags while messages from brave British secret agents, hung from poles, were plucked by wing tips mere inches from the ground. Every circus has its clowns and only a master of his craft can simulate the totally inept. Geoffrey Tyson, that ace of aerobatic clowns, later to be the first to fly the English Channel upside down, brought gasps from the crowd as, with his side slipping, stalling, engine cutting expertise, he flirted with disaster. Local pride was also upheld as one of Aberystwyth's sons, Gwynne Johns, a local ironmonger's clerk and world amateur delayed drop parachute champion, brought to most present their first sight of a man, drifting gently to earth amongst rippling applause.

My sister, four years my senior, had won a free flight in a *Cambrian News* raffle. My appeal for equal treatment was upheld and soon I was sinking into a deep wicker chair, cushioned against the bumps and jolts of taxiing across a cow pasture. The roar of takeoff was deafening, drowning my words of comfort to a terrified mother sitting across the narrow aisle from me. From two hundred feet I saw my home, the garden, the schoolyard. I gazed down, pityingly, at faces turned up towards us from the streets below. The promenade, the beach, the harbour, the fishing boats. Then the return to earth, brushing the tree tops as we did so, to be ejected back amongst the crowd on whom I had so recently looked down with such disdain. The fact that that particular aircraft crashed only weeks later while pioneering in-flight refuelling, killing all on board, was dismissed from the mind of someone so young as to feel he would live for ever.

Then there was the time when Amy Johnson was expected to arrive by car and stay at the Angel Hotel - or so the rumour ran - and she had flown all the way to Australia, alone, in her tiny de Havilland Gipsy Moth, called *Janus*. And she had been the first woman to do it with talk of storms and shark infested seas. And now the words "touring" and "honeymoon" had spread, wagging tongue to wagging tongue, throughout the town. There were only two possible routes into the town and the chances were that they would arrive along Llanbadarn Road which skirted our front garden. For hours I sat on our garden gate with all the patience of the devoted. I imagined the open car, the wave, the smile for her most ardent fan, her hair streaming in the wind - or would she be wearing her leather helmet and goggles?

But she did not come. It had been just that, a rumour; nothing more.

My first excursion out of Wales coincided with my sudden exposure to the Spartan rigours of life in a pre-war English public school. Dedicated, as was the normal practice of that time, to teaching young men how to die well, at the heart of the school was the Officers Training Corps, the OTC, its function to provide gentlemanly officers for the local county regiment. Masters who had sat uneasily at ill fitting desks all week, sprang to life each Saturday, immaculate in Service dress, Sam Browne belts and swagger sticks. But the majority of those khaki clad boys who paraded each Saturday, their boots polished, their belts blancoed, had no wish to be soldiers. They had but one dream - they wanted to fly. Witness to this the record of a school which, at that time, never numbered more than three to four hundred yet won five DSOs and fifteen DFCs.

Witness also the Roll of Honour.

Amongst the names thereon are those of two close, rugby playing friends of mine, Michael "Granny" Good and Jim Taaffe. Granny Good was the pilot of a lumbering Stirling bomber which had clambered into the sky to lay mines off the Kiel Canal, one of three such Stirlings which took off within five minutes of each other, not to return. Jim Taaffe, in a Lancaster bomber, had survived the gruelling trip to bomb a target in northern Italy, only to die, along with thirteen of his comrades, when two exhausted pilots collided on the landing circuit over their home airfield.

To them, Granny and Jim, and to all their brave comrades who died, this book is dedicated.

Chapter One

The chosen site lay between Beacon Hill and Seven Barrows in Hampshire; quintessential English heartland. The time was December 1909, the harvest in, the hedges laid, the rutted ground already firmed by early penetrating frosts. In a land of horse-drawn carts and ploughs, stubble and corn and hay-ricks, the sound of an internal combustion engine was a rarity. Overhead the virginal sky, as yet unsullied by vapour trail, still the undisputed domain of the cawing rook and wheeling buzzard.

Two young men stood close together, another, in thoughtful pose, some distance away. Still further off a fourth, older man, struggled to hide his fear from a young boy, clutching his hand. One of the two, close together, reached into his pocket to withdraw his handerkerchief. He held it between finger and thumb at arm's length. They had tried the smoke, drifting from the end of a cigarette, but that had proved too sensitive. They had agreed that, should the handkerchief blow more than five degrees from the vertical, then they would call it off. At the same time they did not want to see it hanging there, limp. That would not serve their purpose either. It moved, fluttering in the gentlest of breezes. But from what direction did it blow? That was of equal importance. The field sloped slightly downwards, perfect for what they had in mind. They turned their faces into the breeze, equalising its feel on both cheeks, to find it blew from the lower end of the field. They looked at each other and nodded. No one will ever know how much their excitement was tempered by the knowledge that they could no longer find any excuse to put the moment off.

One of the pair moved to climb aboard a man made contraption as exotic to rural England as it was possible to be. In high stiff collar and tie and crumpled suit, his baggy cloth cap turned about, its peak streamlined across his neck, he clambered up to sit in a small wicker basket chair. He was about to fly an aeroplane he, with some help from his friend, had built himself. The fact that he had never seen an aeroplane fly did not deter him.

No safety straps, no windscreen. All he could see in front of him were the rudimentary elevators. Behind him was an engine, laid transversely, driving two pusher propellers. The 36 foot biplane wingspan and what passed for a fuselage consisted of a white wood frame, held together with piano wire. Stretched over all was doped cotton fabric, lovingly sewn together on a Singer machine by his newly wed wife, Louie. The whole rested on bicycle wheels. There was a fixed tailplane but no fin. On his left was a lever that worked the elevators. Move that backwards and forwards and he should go up or down. On his right was a lever for the rudder. Backwards or forwards to turn right or left. At his feet was a bar controlling ailerons which would droop and drag until blown horizontal by the wind. That was how he would bank one way or the other. The propellers were steel tubing to which were clamped aluminium blades. All built from an image in the mind's eye without one working drawing.

Simple really. If some Americans called Wright had done it six years before, this Englishman was going to do it. The engine and taxiing trials had gone well; all that was left now was to take to the air. The fuel supply was ensured, the magneto circuit switched on, one of the propellers swung. The engine coughed into life in a blue haze. The elderly man at the fringe, unable to watch any further, retired to a nearby shed, taking his youngest son with him.

The plane began to move, trundling downhill. With full power, it began to hurtle along at 10, 15, maybe 20 miles per hour. Who knows how fast? Who had heard of a tachometer?

It was now or never. Pulling hard with his left hand, totally ignorant of what physical power was required, the pilot suddenly found himself staring into the pale blue of a winter sky as the plane became almost vertical. At about 15 feet, with a snapping, splitting, tearing sound, a wing failed. Within seconds, a dream lay in shattered fragments. The onlookers raced in fear towards the wreckage, only to find the pilot, one propeller still rotating lazily above his head, already analysing where he had gone wrong, what should be corrected the next time.

Geoffrey de Havilland was that sort of man.

Born in 1882, the son of a village curate, Geoffrey de Havilland, destined to design some of the world's finest aircraft, could have chosen his father better. Fascinated from an early age with all things mechanical, Geoffrey would have little help, financial or intellectual, from the impoverished Vicar of Nuneaton, an unpractical, at times violently irascible man of the mind. But in his mother he had been more fortunate. Before her marriage she had known a life of ease and comfort, servants and society.

Geoffrey's grandfather on his mother's side, was one Jason Saunders, a pillar of the local establishment. Born of good yeoman stock, he was a clear-eyed, successful business man; not a man to throw away hard earned money but prepared to back initiative. Mayor of Oxford in 1876, Jason owned and the family lived in a farm called Medley. Fiercely independent himself, Jason ran the farm as far as was humanly possible on a self sufficient basis; a community within a community. It was there amongst his grandfather's blacksmiths, carpenters and wheelwrights that the young Geoffrey learned the rudiments of marrying wood and metal.

Of his two brothers, Ivon, three years his senior, and Hereward, 12 years his junior, Ivon shared Geoffrey's passion for the burgeoning world of mechanics, though he differed in that it was the application of electrical power that fascinated him.

Educated at St. Edward's School in Oxford, Geoffrey's first engine was a stationary steam engine, purchased for one shilling. Nothing too unusual about that. Most young boys with a mechanical turn of mind had their "donkey" engine with its boiler and methylated spirit lamp, cylinder, piston and flywheel. But Geoffrey, unlike most boys, was not content to leave it there. Next came a small boat with a marine steam engine. In conjunction with Ivon, he went on to design and build a boiler, steam engine and dynamo to give electric light.

Then came the defining moment in young Geoffrey's life.

We live now in an age when most will have travelled in some form of mechanical transport long before their memories serve them. It is difficult therefore to imagine the feelings of two young men, passionately interested, experiencing the sensation of being propelled by an internal combustion engine for the first time. It was the turn of the century, the very sight of a car a rarity. The car involved was a 3.5 HP Benz. Its power transmission, by means of leather bands, slipped on breasting the slightest of gradients but the fact that the two young men had frequently to get out and push failed to dampen their enthusiasm. For one at least, it only confirmed his decision. The beckoning world of mechanical transport in one form or another was becoming irresistible.

With his grandfather's help, Geoffrey entered the Crystal Palace Engineering School while Ivon went off to become an electrical engineer. At Crystal Palace, Geoffrey learned the rudiments of machining and fitting. Whilst there, he built his first real internal combustion engine, a 1.5 HP motor cycle engine. From Crystal Palace he moved to a firm of turbine engineers where he built his second motor bike engine, this time to his own design. Next came the drawing office of the Wolseley car factory, a tyro draughtsman, learning the art of engine design.

In the meanwhile, Ivon had died of flu.

In 1908 - he was now 26 - Geoffrey made a decision, the basis for which he himself would probably have had difficulty in explaining. He would build an aeroplane; this in spite of never having seen one. A.V. Roe had just become the first Englishman to fly over English soil but, five years before, somewhere in distant America, at a place called Kitty Hawk, in the Kill Devil Hills of North Carolina, two brothers called Wright had achieved sustained flight under mechanical power. Bags of gas, with engines attached, had been flying since 1900 but the Wright brothers had achieved this in a proper aeroplane. By 1904 they had even flown in a circle. And now they had brought their plane to France, to Le Mans. France - not England. In November 1906, Albert Santos-Dumont, a wealthy Brazilian, had been the first man to fly in Europe but he had chosen to do this in France. France, without doubt, was ahead of the game, enough of a stimulus for any red blooded Englishman. Henri Farman had already stayed aloft for 30 minutes, flying a one kilometre circuit with his brilliant innovation, the aileron. Admittedly the Farman brothers were sons of English journalists, living abroad, but the names of Voisin and Brequet and Nieuport were also being bandied about and, in August 1909, an aviation week in Reims, La Grande Semaine d'Aviation de la Champagne, attended by the highest echelons of society and politics, had fired a nation's imagination. Farman had flown 112 miles, speeds of 46 miles per hour had been achieved, heights of 500 feet attained. French aviators, still mostly dashing, wealthy young sportsmen, had become the nation's icons, idolised by women. There were even plans for some Frenchman, called Bleriot, to fly cross the English Channel. Drake and Nelson must have been turning in their graves.

Geoffrey went to his grandfather and put his case. The response, one thousand pounds, astonished Geoffrey even though the businessman shone through the generosity as Geoffrey was warned that it would be deducted from his inheritance should Jason die before seeing any return on his money. Now financially solvent, it did not take Geoffrey long to realise he could not do it on his own. Enter Frank Hearle, a marine engineer, who, while Geoffrey began work on a four cylinder, 50 HP engine, taught himself how to make an airframe, to Geoffrey's design, out of wood, fabric and wire. There followed days, weeks and months of industry, based on visions, hopes and dreams that were destined to end in a field in Hampshire, in that pile of twisted metal, splintered wood and torn fabric.

But de Havilland had picked himself up, literally, determined his second attempt would not end the same way. As a young boy, de Havilland had read the newspaper reports of Hiram Maxim's attempts to obtain lift from plane surfaces but the changes in design from that first disastrous attempt would be governed more by pure instinct than any mathematical exactitude. At least, this time, he would have the benefit of having seen an aeroplane in flight, having travelled to watch Grahame-White take off from Wormwood Scrubs.

The engine would lie fore and aft with a single pusher propeller, doing away with complicated bevelled gears and saving weight by doing away with the flywheel. The frame would not be of soft white wood this time but of silver spruce and ash, a choice of materials the future significance of which they would have had no way of appreciating. Front and rear elevators would be interconnected to avoid the near vertical ascent that had been at the heart of the previous debacle and the two levers, almost impossible to co-ordinate, would be replaced with a single control stick, the prototype joy stick. A wooden propeller would replace the steel and aluminium. By September 1910, a mere nine months after the first attempt, all was ready once more, this in spite of the shed at Seven Burrows, bought from Moore-Brabazon who had transferred his flying to France, having to be cleared to allow Lord Carnarvon to entertain his shooting party to lunch. De Havilland was invited; Frank Hearle could only watch.

This time, daylight appeared between the wheels and the ground before safely returning to earth. The fact that it truly flew some 20 yards was confirmed by Frank Hearle, lying prone in the grass. Within days de Havilland was covering 400 yards at a height of ten feet, all in secrecy. It was finally, on September 10, 1910, that a quarter mile flight was reported to the public. Soon quarter mile flights became commonplace with circuits progressing to figures of eight. In doing so, de Havilland was admitted to that small band of adventurers who taught themselves to fly; able to rub shoulders with the likes of the Wrights, Bleriot, Roe, Dunne, Moore-Brabazon, Rolls, Grahame-White and Cody. Gaining in confidence, his first passenger was an ecstatic Frank Hearle, soaring to 100 feet, and it was not long before his wife, their eight month old child, Geoffrey, in her arms, flew alongside him.

So; he had an aeroplane and he could fly it. But what now? Geoffrey de Havilland was not the sort of man to rest on his laurels. Flying and the construction of aircraft he knew was to be his life. But he had a wife and young family to support, not to mention the small matter of financial backing. He could not expect his grandfather to put more money into a project that so far had provided nothing more than joyriding for his grandson and his friends.

But where could he turn?

Chapter Two

On the second of July, 1900, LZ1, the first Zeppelin, lifted into the air. By 1906, one of its successors had flown non-stop for 24 hours. Probably the finest, LZ70, 740 feet long with a ceiling of 16,000 feet, would have a range of 7,500 miles. The furthest rocky outpost of the British Isles would fall within its compass. But Britain, confident in the invincibility of its Royal Navy and the power of its professional Army, largely ignored the possibility of being vulnerable from the air. That science-fiction chap, H.G. Wells, had published, back in 1907, his book, *The War in the Air*, with its fantastic stories of whole cities being rased to the ground from the air. Some delegates at the Hague Peace Conference that same year must have read it as they voted to ban all bombing of open cities. But who really believed such nonsense? So long as Admiral Fisher with his Dreadnoughts could protect their shores, what did the British public have to fear? In 1909, R.P. Hearne, in his book *Aerial Warfare*, told them. His description of an aerial attack on London sent an anxious shiver through Whitehall. London, Hearne claimed, was at the mercy of the Zeppelin, that Britain, as things stood, had no credible defence. Dreadnoughts were no protection from bombs raining down from ten thousand feet. People in high places began to agree. Lord Montague of Beaulieu, writing in *The Times*, reminded the readers of Lord Northcliffe's statement that England was no longer an island. Bleriot's peaceful crossing of the English Channel in July the same year, praised by some as a sublime example of international bonding, may also have been seen in a different light by slowly awakening military strategists.

  Faced with such a situation, Britain did what it does best; it formed a committee. In April, the Prime Minister, Herbert Asquith created the Advisory Committee for Aeronautics. He was fortunate to have as his Secretary of State for War a man of high intelligence.

R.B. Haldane, a brilliant lawyer and philosopher, was no scientist but he knew a good one when he saw one and made sure that Lord Rayleigh, Nobel Prize winner for Physics and future President of the Royal Society, was appointed President of the new committee. Seven out of ten of its Members were Fellows of the Royal Society, their first duty - to take stock.

Britain, in its characteristically amateurish fashion, had its own balloon programme. In fact, in earlier days it had led the world in the military application of balloons, using them extensively for observation in the South African campaign. There had been a balloon at the siege of Ladysmith - until it ran out of gas. Colonel James Templer, his waxed moustache and jaunty pill box hat much in evidence, had returned from his brush with the Boers with a reputation and had been posted to command the Government Balloon Factory at Aldershot, later, in 1905, to be transferred to a place called Farnborough, deep in sleepy, rural England. An honest, thoroughly trustworthy man, he nevertheless had become a victim of a power struggle to gain control of the balloons. Sir John French, at that time Commander-in-Chief, Aldershot, by devious, rather dishonourable means, had made life at Farnborough intolerable for Templer, forcing him into early retirement, to be replaced as Superintendent in 1906 by one of French's men, Colonel J.E. Capper. The change of site and the disruption in command had led to a decline in design and engineering standards so that British balloons now paled into insignificance alongside the Zeppelin.

Even so, Londoners had had their first sight of a British airship when *Nulli Secundus 1* had flown over St Paul's Cathedral in October 1907, only for it to be destroyed by its own creators when it threatened to break loose from its moorings in a high wind. And, in 1910, a year after the formation of the Advisory Committee, a successor, *Beta 1*, was happily taking part in military manoeuvres.

It was going to require firm but diplomatic handling if the whole thrust of aeronautical research was going to alter course. After all, the airship, of which the Zeppelin was the supreme example, was still considered to be the weapon of the future. Where could they find a man with such talents as to replace harmoniously the proud old soldier with the bright young scientist? For it was decided; Britain would not try to catch up on airships, where the Germans were in a different class, but perhaps concentrate on those new fangled flying machines. But where was such a man to be found?

Mervyn Joseph Pius O'Gorman was an ebullient, flamboyant, forthrightly generous Irishman. He had studied Engineering and French in Dublin and had obtained his City and Guilds Diplomas in Physics. After working in France, he had returned to a flourishing London consultancy in the booming car industry. From this he was wooed away to Farnborough by Haldane and Rayleigh, first with a part time contract - a few days a week. Soon he was to give Farnborough his total commitment, beginning to charm his way around the soldiers. He might have expected resentment from the man he was to replace as Superintendent, Colonel Capper, and it says a great deal for O'Gorman's personality that all went smoothly, O'Gorman allowing Capper, a balloonist to the core, to play with *Beta 1* while he, O'Gorman, got on with the job of producing aeroplanes.

He now began the task of building a team of brilliant young scientists that was to stand the country in good stead in the war that loomed. First he chose his Chief Engineer, Major F.M. Green. His first choice as designer and pilot would probably have been the brilliant young Rolls, had he not been killed flying in an airshow earlier that year. But Green, during his apprenticeship, had worked with an equally brilliant young man who had impressed him immensely, one Geoffrey de Havilland. By chance, they met once more in November at an aero show at Olympia. They talked and Green went back to his boss. De Havilland had his own aeroplane, had built it himself to his own design, had learned to fly with it. Just the sort of man O'Gorman was looking for, Green argued. O'Gorman agreed, offering de Havilland a job at Farnborough, now renamed the Army Aircraft Factory, on one condition, that he brought his aeroplane with him, provided, of course, it had completed the one hour flight required before acceptance. Satisfied, O'Gorman paid £400 for the aircraft, and de Havilland moved into Farnborough, also on one condition, that Frank Hearle went with him as his mechanic. One of O'Gorman's problems was solved. He was shrewd enough almost certainly to know he had solved de Havilland's problem also.

And so, as 1911 began, de Havilland found himself where perhaps fate had always intended he should be, one of Britain's pioneer explorers in this new and exciting dimension, a position he was to hold with dignity and distinction for over 50 years. They were heady times. To the sheer thrill of flying was added the piquancy of chauvinistic international competition. The Americans had begun it all with Orville and Wilbur Wright - it had even been claimed that fellow American, Samuel Pierpont Langley, with a one horse power steam engine, had flown three-quarters of a mile as early as 1896 - but it was the French, those French with their damned élan, who were carrying everything before them. Wilbur Wright was now doing his flying in France, having had his invention refused by the US War Department, wary of these new fangled flying machines after investing a great deal of money in Langley's earlier failures. Capper had met the Wrights at the St Louis World Fair as long before as 1904 and begged them to sell their patent to Britain but, despite Capper's pleadings, the Wrights' applications were again turned down, twice by the British War Office, once by the Admiralty. Most British flyers were learning to fly in France. Even Moore-Brabazon, holder of the Royal Aero Club's first certificate, had defected. Admittedly, another American, the colourful, incomparable Colonel Cody of Birdville, Texas, had come to Britain, to Farnborough, to fly. Just before de Havilland's arrival, Cody, originally employed as the chief instructor in kiting, had won the Michelin Prize by flying 186 miles - but in a French machine. Claude Grahame-White, on his way to winning the Gordon Bennet Cup Race in the USA, had probably done more than anyone to spur an interest in aviation in that vast nation by an Englishman flying a French machine, landing in the street outside the White House to pay his respects to President Taft. The Voisin brothers, Charles and Gabriel, had become the aircraft manufacturers to the wealthy, Bleriot was selling his planes as fast as he could make them and Henri Farman had just established an endurance record, covering 288 miles in over eight hours. Such was French supremacy that any plane with a tractor propeller, including those built in Britain, would belong to the series BE - Bleriot Experimentals. Both the plane that de Havilland had brought to Farnborough with him and the first plane he constructed there had pusher propellers. That being so, despite the fact that they were designed by an Englishman, built by an Englishman, flown by an Englishman, it was required they be referred to as FE1 and FE2 - Farman Experimentals. This was perhaps the ultimate humiliation.

Where was British pride?

It would be another four years before de Havilland's third plane would fly but at least it would have the dignity of being designated DH1.

In those early, stumbling months of 1911, when, in February, an Army Order was issued, creating the Air Battalion of the Royal Engineers, and, in April, the Balloon Factory became the Army Aircraft Factory, de Havilland found himself to all intents and purposes Farnborough's sole test pilot and designer. The illiterate Cody, happiest flying planes constructed by others, just so long as it did not interfere with his cowboy acts on the music halls, had already moved on. For a year or so, de Havilland was his own boss, though restricted in that the construction of aircraft, as opposed to balloons and kites, was still officially forbidden. It required collusion on the part of O'Gorman and Green to give de Havilland's creative genius free rein, allowing such liberal "reconstruction" of planes brought in from outside for repair as to render the end results unrecognisable as the planes that had arrived. One such plane, a Voisin donated to the War Office by the Duke of Westminster and brought to Farnborough for repairs, was given to de Havilland for "reconstruction" and the BE1 was born. This plane, though never put into production, survived multiple crashes to become the standard bearer of its type and was last seen flying at the Central Flying School in July 1916. Creative and practical, a pure scientist at peace with his own world, protected and supported by O'Gorman and Green, men he respected utterly, de Havilland was a happy man.

But all that was about to change. Serious matters were afoot. de Havilland was about to lose his position centre stage, shouldered out into the wings as heavyweights, both military and political, vied for the limelight.

Winston Churchill, now First Lord of the Admiralty, was already taking a keen interest in aviation, pressing for the formation of a new corps of airmen. Asquith, the Prime Minister, who probably knew as little about aviation as the man in the street, was obliged to form another committee, the two key members of which were quick to see in Farnborough a stage on which they might further their careers. O'Gorman might be the stage manager, de Havilland the brilliant scriptwriter and designer but there was no doubt who intended to be the leading players - Brigadier David Henderson and Staff Captain Frederick Sykes. And backstage, waiting, as yet unaware of the role he was to play, was a man called Trenchard.

David Henderson, a quietly tenacious Scot, was fortunate in having two attributes, often found to be incompatible in one man, practicality and intelligence. Obtaining a university degree in engineering had not precluded him from being a fine pianist. His pastime was song writing. Despite his artistry, there was no doubting his manhood. As head of Kitchener's intelligence team in South Africa, he had been in action against the Zulus in 1884 and had been present at the Battle of Omdurman in 1898. If further proof was needed, he could always show his wounds, sustained at Ladysmith in 1900. He also possessed all the social graces that, together with his military record, would ensure an illustrious career in the Army. Final confirmation of that early promise came in 1904 when the War Office published his highly successful textbook on Field Intelligence, *The Art of Reconnaissance*. A rising star, he was searching for his place in the military firmament. Farnborough would do nicely. He had already seen, as so many thrusting young officers had seen, that a pair of wings, stitched to a khaki uniform, did no harm. Driven perhaps more by ambition than the thrill of soaring aloft, he learned how to fly, at 49 the oldest pilot of his day. There is little record of his flying subsequently, returning as he did to the War Office as Director of Military Training.

Frederick Sykes was born in Croydon in 1877 and enlisted during the Boer War as a humble trooper in the Imperial Yeomanry

Scouts. Such was his innate ability, however, that he soon found himself commissioned into Lord Roberts' Bodyguard. In 1901 he received the soldiers mark of honour, a serious wound, and, on returning to Britain, was granted a regular commission in a fashionable regiment, the 15th Hussars. Part of his service in India was spent at the Staff College in Quetta where he must have impressed as, on his return to Britain, obviously an intellectual cut above his brother officers, he was promoted Major and appointed General Staff Officer to the Directorate of Operations at the War Office, a backwater far from the promotional mainstream. He had to get out and possessed the vision to see the opportunities the aeroplane presented. But, unlike Henderson, his flying lessons at Brooklands were not prompted purely by ambition. Years before, genuinely fascinated by man's struggle to fly, he had been seconded to a Royal Engineer unit involved with balloons and man-lifting kites. In 1904, when home on leave from West Africa, he had made several balloon ascents and had passed an examination in ballooning - at Farnborough. He, like Henderson, was an intelligent man, at odds to maintain a balance between the man of action and the man of thought. Whereas, in Henderson, the soldier probably came first, the artist subdued, Sykes was more the university don than the soldier, described as "... too cold to secure affection, too calculating to inspire enthusiasm." Perhaps a kinder appraisal would be a courageous man but somewhat too devious and reflective to be totally effective.

And the third man?

Hugh Montague Trenchard, the son of an officer in the King's Own Yorkshire Light Infantry, was born in Taunton in 1873 and was commissioned into the Royal Scots Fusiliers at the age of 20. To understand the man, it is necessary to follow his path between these two momentous occasions. He received no formal primary education, having a resident tutor for whom he showed no respect. Sent to prep school at the age of 10, while openly boasting of his academic limitations, he showed early signs of traits, more obvious in later life, that included a tendency to hero worship and a total disinclination to learn from anyone. From prep school he joined Hammonds, the select crammer for the Royal Naval College at Dartmouth - and failed the entry examination. If the Navy would not have him, perhaps the Army would. His career at an Army crammer, run by a gentle, benign man of the cloth Trenchard also despised, was chequered. Captain of the First XV, he was suddenly removed and ostracised when his father was declared bankrupt, to return only as a result of charity from family friends. A big, strong young man, undoubtedly affected by such humiliation, he became not so much withdrawn as gruff, angry and inscrutable. His twice attempted entry into the Royal Military Academy at Woolwich met the same fate as at Dartmouth. Finally he gained entry to the Regular Army via the back door, passing the entry examination to the Militias - at his third attempt. Eighth from the bottom of the Infantry List, a glittering military career was launched.

Finally embraced by the Army, he was sent to India where he won the All India Rifle Shooting Competition and became expert at polo and horse racing. His first contact with Lt Winston Churchill of the 4th Hussars, both physical and acrimonious as it was, occurred on the polo field. Transferred to fight the Boers, he was shot through one lung and survived; no mean feat given the times. Lured by the Boers into an ambush at a farm in Western Transvaal, it was perhaps in keeping with the man that he was cut down, charging the farmhouse's front door across open ground. Invalided home, half paralysed from the waist down and with a partially collapsed lung, he was sent to St Moritz to convalesce. As indifferent to his own injuries as he was disparaging about sickness in others, within days of his arrival he was hurtling out of control down the Cresta Run on a toboggan. Each fall he sustained only spurred him on, declaring his weak legs much improved after a particularly serious accident. As if to prove his point, he entered for and won the Beginner's and Freshmen's Cresta Run Cup.

Returning to South Africa he led an unsuccessful raid to capture the Boer Government yet still managed to impress Lord Kitchener. And why not? He was, after all, a soldier's soldier, a military man, through and through. Released from the necessity for academic achievement - he read only biographies in his search for heroes - revelling in the spartan physical aspects of army life, he became supremely self confident. Blunt and uncompromising, to be heartily disliked by his colleagues was, to him, no more than a sign that he was heading in the right direction. But fate was to take a hand. Just as he was beginning to make a name for himself, war, so essential for military ambitions, ended. Back in Britain, offers of his services to the Mounted Branch of the Colonial Defence Force, to the Egyptian Army, even to the Macedonian International Gendarmerie, were declined. For the best part of 10 years, Trenchard was to disappear reluctantly into the African hinterland as Lieutenant Colonel (Temporary), Commanding Officer of the Southern Nigerian Regiment. Tired of subduing troublesome natives, he returned to Britain, a 39-year-old major with only one fully functioning lung and distinctly limited military prospects. Looking around, he too saw the possibilities presented to a thoroughly military man amongst the ranks of disorganised, ill disciplined, amateurish flyers. He might not be very bright but he was not *that* stupid. A stubborn mind, uncluttered by too many original thoughts, can still show surprising powers of perception. He too must learn to fly.

The total sum of these three men's ultimate aeronautical

expertise would never match one tenth that of de Havilland. Yet, as so often happens, men of ambition, seeking power with a gift for political intrigue, would fight to control and command the inventive spirit that had made their positions possible in the first place. And, as in the human child, where attitudes and beliefs, engrained by dogma in the formative years, are difficult, sometimes impossible to eradicate in later life, the battle of personalities between these three men would leave its mark on the new born military force. The infant air force inevitably would inherit the characteristics of that personality which would prove the dominant. Which one would it be?

1912 was to prove the defining year in the lives of young men in their flying machines and in the careers of those who would control them. In January, the Army could muster just 11 actual flyers, the Navy no more than eight. The French possessed over 250. Henderson had been picked out by Asquith and Rayleigh as their man to head this still rather nebulous armed force and Sykes had already progressed to being a member of the Committee for Imperial Defence. Both hankered after Farnborough.

While Henderson prowled, watchfully, under the aegis of the Advisory Committee for Aeronautics, Sykes, now promoted to Major, busied himself on the Committee for Imperial Defence, striving for an air force independent of an Army who viewed the flyers as no more than another cavalry corps under its command. Major Sykes won the day and, on April 13, 1912, a Royal Warrant was issued and the Royal Flying Corps formed, consisting of Military and Naval Wings and a Central Flying School. Henderson realised his dream of overall command while Sykes was promoted lieutenant colonel to command the Military Wing - at Farnborough.

One of the Central Flying School's earliest pupils was Hugh "Boom" Trenchard. If he could win the Cresta Run, he could learn to fly. Given 10 days to do so by the War Office - any longer and he would have been over age - his flying course lasted all of 13 days, one hour fourteen minutes of which he spent in the air in a Maurice Farman. Rated "an indifferent flyer" when receiving his certificate in August, it was only in keeping with the man that, by October, he had been made an instructor. Less than a year later, he would be Assistant Commandant!

By the autumn of 1912, the basic structure of the future air force was beginning to take shape. The two services saw the aeroplane in different lights and, with the powerful backing of the First Lord of the Admiralty, Winston Churchill, the Navy shunned the Aircraft Factory and its Government planes, favouring private companies such as Shorts. Inevitably the Naval Wing, with little in common traditionally with the Military, went its own way, eventually, in July 1914, to become the Royal Naval Air Service, leaving the soldiers to their own devices. Though far more prestigious committees met at the War Office, it was at Farnborough, in the form of a small triumvirate sub-committee of the CID that the technical problems were being tackled, the future strategic philosophy formulated. The three men were Brigadier General David Henderson, Colonel Frederick Sykes and Major Duncan Macanese, a workaholic patriot who was to die of exhaustion before the Armistice and leave his friends to attain high office.

And how did de Havilland react, the pure scientist suddenly finding himself under military control; a man imbued with the simple love of flying abruptly subservient to men who saw in the aeroplane nothing but an instrument of war? Very favourably, it would seem. While Henderson busied himself in the background,

Sykes and de Havilland struck up a particularly close relationship. De Havilland's next plane, the BE2, a modification of a reconstruction of a Voisin, had first flown in February and was now proving very reliable, if rather slow, and Sykes, who described his years in command of the Military Wing as amongst the happiest of his life, seems to have spent more time as de Havilland's passenger on long cross-country flights in the BE2 than flying himself. During the year, Sykes was a passenger when de Havilland, in an endurance flight of three and a half hours, claimed a British altitude record of over 10,000 feet. On another occasion they soared aloft together in their trusty BE2 to 9,500 feet in no more than one hour and 20 minutes. Henderson, Sykes and Macanese might not have been instinctive designers and pilots but they were intelligent, thoughtful men. To them fell the responsibility of deciding to what military purpose these fascinating, beguiling contraptions of wood, steel and fabric were best suited?

The embryo fighting force was still part of the Army, commanded and staffed by khaki clad army officers, steeped in army tradition and ways of thinking. While the potential for subduing fractious tribesmen in far-flung colonial outposts had not escaped their attention, to the military mind the aeroplane could have but one logical function, reconnaissance; airborne light cavalry. They would probably have come to this conclusion whoever had been in ultimate command. With Henderson, the expert on intelligence gathering in the field, in such a position of power and influence, it became irresistible. Sykes agreed wholeheartedly, making the decision inevitable. Admittedly some Italian, a Lieutenant Gavotti, had already dropped some home-made bombs on some Turks, but visions of bombing as yet did not amount to more than lobbing a few hand grenades over the side, concepts of aerial combat a few pot-shots with revolver or Lee Enfield. No;

what was needed was a mobile observation platform to report on troop movements behind the enemy lines. Speed was to be a secondary consideration, stability all important. Accurate observation would be difficult if the slightest accidental twitch of the controls sent a pilot fighting for his life. There was little doubt there were faster planes than the BE2 out there but what the War Office required was a plane easily flown by the average pilot, not a racer favoured by the daredevil, private adventurer. Accordingly, the War Office forbad their flyers to compete against privately owned planes. But Sykes knew the plane, respected de Havilland's ability, and recommended that the BE2 be put into full-scale production for the war that loomed ever closer. Henderson was taken for a flight, was impressed and gave his approval. The first Victoria Cross to be won in the air would be in a BE2.

In the final run-up to the Great War, those tense, exciting two years, 1912 to 1914, the world of British aviation was divided, at times bitterly, into two camps. Private enterprise, dependent on rich, daredevil young men to purchase their planes, looked with disdain on the Royal Aircraft Factory where, from the outside, little appeared to be happening. To some extent this was true, due mainly to restrictive bureaucracy and the continuing drain on resources of balloon research. As a result, neither of the planes the Aircraft Factory sent to war had originated within it. The BE2 was a reconstructed, modified Voisin and the FE2 was still essentially that plane de Havilland had brought with him to Farnborough. But the BE2 would serve the RFC well and the FE2, several versions of which would be built, would find its niche. The tractor propeller of the BE2 was more efficient, obviously the design of the future, but, without a gun synchronised to fire through it, the field of fire was restricted. The FE2 however, as a pusher, had a ready-made gun platform at the nose, capable of firing Lewis guns, Maxims or even a Vickers one pound quick firing gun. Well into 1917, it would be dropping its bombs and firing its guns, the last direct descendents of that plane that had inched de Havilland into the air at Seven Barrows.

While the two sides of British aviation bickered - aircraft from the Aircraft Factory were allowed to appear at air shows but discouraged from competing - in France Bleriot, Farman and Gnome prospered. Virtually every British plane that went to war did so with a French engine. De Havilland's free spirit was reined in further as, now a 2nd lieutenant in the Special Reserve, he came under the direct command of Henderson. In March 1913, shortly before Cody was killed, he was involved in a major crash, only to survive with a fractured jaw. Later that year, he was to lose his friend and mechanic, Frank Hearle, amicably, as Hearle left to marry de Havilland's sister, Ione. But the low point in de Havilland's time at Farnborough was still to come. It arrived in the form of an order from Henderson, something about which his guardian angels, Sykes, O'Gorman and Green could do nothing. Henderson was now all powerful, appointed in September 1913 Director General of the Directorate of Military Aeronautics. Brigadier General Henderson decided he needed an Inspector of Aircraft to supervise his Aeronautical Inspection Directorate. Who better to fill such a post than that bright young man at Farnborough - 2nd Lieutenant de Havilland; the perfect choice. Transplanted from design office to committee room, desperately unhappy, de Havilland did the only thing open to him - he resigned and went over to the other side. In May 1914, antagonising a very powerful man as he did so, he turned his back on Farnborough to join Holt Thomas's design team at Edgware. At Airco, he breathed again.

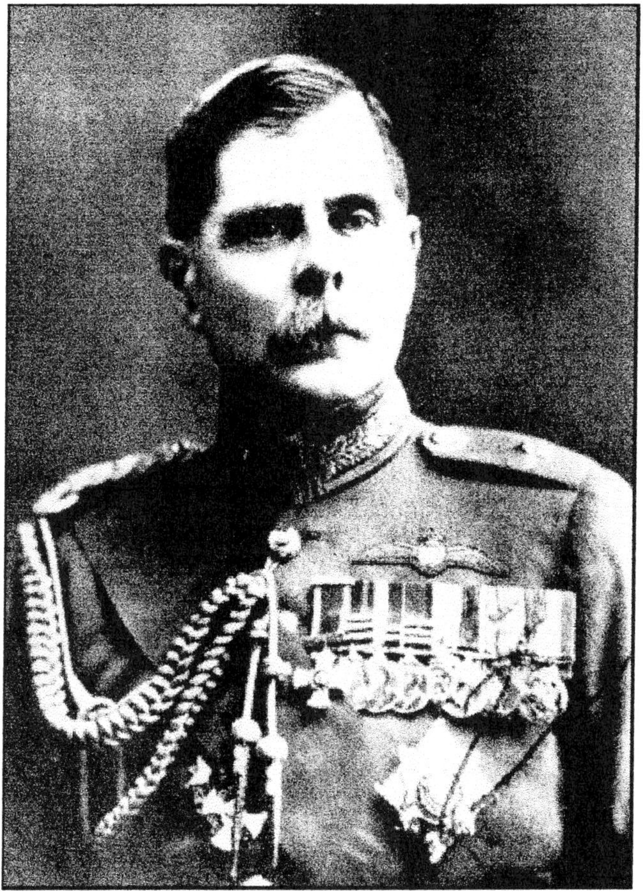

Chapter Three

And so, on August 4, 1914, they went to war, hurrying not to miss the sport that everyone, well, nearly everyone - Lord Kitchener, Secretary of State for War, was not convinced - confidently predicted would be "over by Christmas". They did so with the patriotic zeal only to be expected of such a dashing, adventurous breed of men. Their commanders, governors of their fate, slotted in at their head. Henderson, promoted to Major General, would have overall command of the RFC in France; Colonel Sykes would be his second in command and Chief of Staff. Trenchard, champing at the bit, would be left to exercise his considerable ability to organise in command of the Military Wing at Farnborough.

And 2nd Lieutenant Geoffrey de Havilland, that gifted aircraft designer? He found himself on fruitless anti-submarine patrols out of remote Montrose.

The RFC took with them to France some four squadrons, a motley group of 63 assorted BE2s, Farmans, Avros and Bleriots, to face a German airforce of 10 airships and 245 aircraft, for the most part stolid, stable reconnaissance planes. The bulk of the force flew to Amiens on the 13th, just in time to meet the ground forces in full retreat from Mons, and Sykes, convinced of a brief, triumphant war, committed his total force, including reserves, with no heed for the morrow.

It was only a matter of days before aircraft, for the first time in history, materially affected the conduct of war. The few hand-grenades and fire-bombs that the intrepid flyers hurled down on the advancing German hordes could hardly be expected to stop them in their tracks but it was British aerial reconnaissance that gave the French advance warning of German dispositions and led to their decision to stand and fight on the Marne, thereby saving Paris and forcing the Germans to begin digging trenches that were to scar the fair face of Flanders for the next four years.

Among those carrying out the reconnaissance was Captain Philip Joubert de la Ferte of 3 Squadron. Destined to survive the war and reach high rank, his acute perception of his commanders, viewed from the cutting edge of battle, would prove revealing. Another young man, involved in the early reconnaissance and destined for power and influence in later years, was fortunate to survive the first few weeks. Wilfrid Freeman and his observer crashed behind the enemy lines but managed to avoid capture, survived being shelled by what is now euphemistically described as "friendly fire" and finally returned to base by swimming the Aisne. Fate had obviously decided he was required for greater things.

By October, as the Battle for Ypres began, it was becoming obvious to all that it was going to be a long, hard struggle and Henderson and Sykes had cause to rue their early profligacy in men and machines. Depleted reserves made replacement of losses difficult. This did not prevent Trenchard, back at home, from openly criticising Henderson and Sykes for "wrapping their machines and pilots in cotton wool". A soldier to the last, in the mould of Kitchener, Haig and French, he campaigned hard to bring the RFC under the direct command of the Army but was overruled by Henderson and Sykes. Even so, the RFC soon found itself divided into three Wings, one for each of the Army Corps, with one Headquarters Wing, nominally for strategic reconnaissance but, in practice, to maintain overall command in Henderson's hands.

Trenchard's nagging discontent at Farnborough finally brought its reward. He was offered the command of No. 1 Wing in France, an offer he gladly accepted but with one proviso; he would accept commands from Henderson and Henderson alone. Under no circumstances would he take orders from Sykes whom he despised, referring to him as that "most conceited and indecisive staff officer". Given this assurance, Trenchard left for France and, while he had had little time to stamp his authority on Farnborough, he must be credited with at least one astute move. It was due to his influence that Geoffrey de Havilland was promoted to Captain, brought back from Scotland and seconded to Airco with orders to build bombers, bombers and more bombers.

By the closing weeks of 1914, as the RFC showed all the signs of settling into what was generally accepted as its role, that of the Army's airborne cavalry, Henderson began to tire, hankering after a return to a command in the field, a wish no doubt strengthened by the eternal sniping between Sykes and Trenchard below him. In due course he had his way, being given command of the Army's 1st Division, thus leaving a power vacuum in his wake.

There followed an astonishing train of events that would have unimaginable long-term consequences.

Years later, de la Ferte, who thought Trenchard resembled Kitchener in many ways, would write of his erstwhile commander as "... blunt to the point of rudeness, intolerant of human weakness and indecision, averse to politics and intrigue and single of purpose". Nevertheless, while far from impressed with Trenchard's intellectual ability, Ferte had come to "... respect his integrity, his drive and his extraordinary power of coming to a correct conclusion by a complicated and sometimes erroneous series of arguments." But Sykes, not Trenchard, was now the logical successor to Henderson as General Officer Commanding the RFC in France and there was no means by which Trenchard could stomach that. Behind everyone's back, Trenchard appealed to Kitchener, his old mentor in his days in South Africa, threatening that, if Sykes were to be given command, he, Trenchard, would immediately resign and return to his old regiment, the Royal Scots Fusiliers. Kitchener advised Haig to return Henderson to the RFC. While Haig dithered, reluctant to lose such an accomplished field commander, Sykes, seeing a glittering prize being snatched from his clasp, did a bit of his own lobbying. He too had friends at the War Office, albeit not as powerful as Kitchener, dating back to his days on the Directorate of Operations. Darkly, he hinted at good reasons why Henderson should not return. Kitchener finally resolved the problem, countermanding Henderson's transfer and returning him to his original command. Retribution followed. Within months, Sykes had been placed "at the disposal of the Admiralty", effectively removed from the Army, ultimately to be banished to command a small air service unit in the Dardanelles. When Sykes left, Henderson offered Trenchard his job; but Trenchard refused. Such was his level of self belief now that being second in command to anyone did not appeal. Now there was no one of consequence standing between Trenchard and Henderson and the command Trenchard coveted and, with no self doubt as to his ability to command, only one appointment was going to tempt him away from No 1 Wing. Not bad for a man so "averse to politics and intrigue". From quelling unruly tribesmen in deepest Africa, to indifferent pupil pilot, to flying instructor, to Assistant Flying School Commandant, to Military Wing Commander, to Commander No. 1 Wing in France; stepping stones founded on boundless physical energy, indifference to personal danger and total self belief.

There remained but one step to go.

In June 1912, George Holt Thomas had first registered his Aircraft Company. For two years he had been happy to build, under licence, Henry and Maurice Farman aircraft. But, as Airco gained valuable manufacturing experience, Thomas had visions of building his own and it had been de Havilland who had convinced him that the first requirement had been a design team. Thomas had promptly offered him the job and de Havilland, now disillusioned and discontented as a mere Inspector at Farnborough, had accepted gladly. Apart from a short period searching for non-existent submarines, he would remain at Airco throughout the war, designing a series of aircraft that Thomas generously allowed to carry his initials. DH1 first flew in January 1915, DH2 in June 1915. Both were successful, some DH2s being still in squadron service two years later. But de Havilland's heart could not have been in the design. Both were "pusher" planes, their propellers behind the cockpit, and de Havilland was convinced that "tractor" planes were to be the aircraft of the future. But the RFC did not possess a machine gun synchronised to fire through the propeller. What was urgently required was a gun platform in the nose and it must be admitted that, despite the danger posed by objects floating out of the cockpit to foul the propeller, often with disastrous results, together with the crew being crushed by the engine in the event of a crash, the DH2 proved superior to the German Fokker E.111 and played its part in ending the "Fokker scourge". DH3, an attempt at a twin 'pusher' engined bomber intended to bomb Berlin was a failure. But creative genius cannot be denied and de Havilland's first tractor aircraft, the DH4, would make his name.

During the first half of 1915, the RFC struggled to find its true role in warfare. The need for reconnaissance sped the development of the aerial camera though photographs, taken before the Battle of Neuve Chapelle, which might have prevented much of the slaughter, were largely ignored by the field commanders. The planes operated singly, unescorted by fighters. The days of the dogfight were yet to dawn. Casualties were high, as many men and machines being lost in crashes as from enemy ground fire. Losses became so severe and well trained replacements so scarce that even Trenchard was obliged for a while to limit his more senior pilots to short distance reconnaissance. If a plane crashed behind the enemy lines it meant the loss of a pilot even if he survived. Such a passive role must have proved very irksome to Trenchard, particularly as the man he had clashed with on the polo field, Winston Churchill, was very differently employed.

Churchill, First Lord of the Admiralty at the outbreak of war, had been one of the first to see the potential of air power. It was no surprise, therefore, that he had made sure the Navy had built its own air force, the Royal Naval Air Service, quite distinct from the Army. When, as early as September 1914, Kitchener, foreseeing a long struggle, had invited Churchill to undertake the defence of the British Isles, Churchill's reaction, imbued as he was with the old infantry dictum that attack is the best form of defence, had been entirely predictable. Having made sure the main Channel ports had not fallen into enemy hands by controversially prolonging the doomed defence of Antwerp, Churchill had promptly despatched RNAS squadrons to Dunkirk. The only threat to mainland Britain, Churchill had concluded, had been the Zeppelin. Once in the air, there had been at that time no effective defence against them. Ergo; they must be destroyed on the ground. The raids by the RNAS on the Zeppelin sheds at Cologne, Dusseldorf and Friedrichshafen were the first truly strategic bombing raids in the history of warfare.

These attacks apart, the general view of air power was still that of Army support. That view was to change dramatically in the early hours of June 1, 1915, the night the first bombs dropped on London. In February, Zeppelins had crossed the North Sea to bomb Yarmouth. But that had been Yarmouth; this was London. When Hauptmann Linnarz in his JZ 38 killed five Londoners, there was a public outcry with a demand for retribution. A wave of fear driven aggression swept the country as memories of R.P. Hearne's description in his book, *Aerial Warfare*, of London at the mercy of the Zeppelin must have come flooding back. H.G. Wells, in a letter to *The Express,* claimed that 2,000 bombers could raze Essen to the ground; that even if 1,000 planes were lost in the process, such sacrifice would compare favourably with that sustained to no avail at Neuve Chapelle. Several Members of Parliament rose in the House to speak in support. At a War Council meeting, it was suggested that Germany's grain crop should be blighted by air attack while O'Gorman favoured burning the crops, a view supported by Winston Churchill who saw blighting as another form of poisoning, something with which he could not agree on moral grounds. The groundswell of fear and anger, directed at the politicians, was transmitted to the Army Commanders. It had lost none of its impetus by the time it reached France and a tired Henderson, a sensitive, compassionate man, coming to the end of a year during which he had had to endure the loss of most of the dashing young men he had brought to France with him, returned to the War Office. Trenchard, promoted to Brigadier General, took his place.

Things were about to change.

During the two years, mid-1915 to mid-1917, Trenchard ruled the RFC with a rod of iron. He was as indifferent to the orders of his political and military masters as he was unresponsive to the advice, wishes and fears of his subordinates. He would not have got away with such obduracy had he not inherited from Henderson Captain Maurice Baring, an inspired appointment as ADC. Baring was everything that Trenchard was not; the fourth son of a Baron, educated at Eton and Trinity College, Cambridge, cultured, a linguist, a journalist, writer and novelist, he was wealthy, artistic and self-effacing. He spent his time supplying Trenchard's intellectual needs, smoothing ruffled feathers, repairing social gaffes. When inspecting a squadron, "Boom" Trenchard, gruff and tetchy, would stride around, trailing overawed commanders in his wake while Baring, faceless amongst the junior ranks, tapped into their fears, their technical problems, their true account of the last sortie. To his credit, Trenchard appreciated what Baring was doing behind the scenes and the two men, poles apart in so many ways, became firm friends.

There appear to have been only two people that Trenchard, for ever in need of heroes, held in high regard; Kitchener and Haig. Kitchener he respected while Haig he revered, calling him "The Chief". It is not surprising therefore that, during those two "backbone" years of the war, all Trenchard's considerable energies were directed to giving support to Haig's efforts to win the war on the ground on the Western Front. To do so, however, the pattern of aerial warfare would need to change. While reconnaissance would remain one of the RFC's important functions, bombing and ground strafing would become increasingly dominant; but only on a tactical scale. The escalating bombing attacks would be carried out in the national interest, in the hope of somehow shortening the war. The governing factor would always be, in what way would this assist the Army. The nearest the bombing came to being strategic in nature were attacks on such targets as rail heads or ammunition dumps behind the German lines, but always with the Army in mind. Even these attacks were rarely concentrated, Trenchard spreading his offensive thinly over a wide area. More often than not, his pilots were left to attack targets of opportunity in what Trenchard termed Distant Offensive Patrols. There was no overall strategic plan, certainly no integration with his allies in the French Air Force whom he considered to "excel in conception but fail in execution".

But while there may be grounds for argument for and against the methods Trenchard used in a tactical sense, it was the ruthless nature of his handling of those under his command that was open to criticism. Utterly inflexible, he simply could not think in terms other than those of relentless offensive. While biographers have struggled, somewhat unconvincingly, to depict Trenchard as a hard man with an assiduously concealed soft, sensitive, compassionate centre, he certainly gave all the appearance of being unaffected by casualty rates that frequently meant a squadron might have over 100 per cent losses in but a few months. Poorly trained, inexperienced young pilots, casualty replacements, were thrown into battle with no thought of pausing to build up strength and morale. Losses caused by his obsession with unrelenting offensive resulted in his having to recruit Naval pilots, taken reluctantly from their long-range bombing attacks which Trenchard saw as no more than a diversion from where he saw the war being won, on the battlefield.

In 1916 Trenchard was determined to go on the offensive in parallel with Haig who was planning his "big push". Casualties soared as Trenchard lost 20 per cent of his entire force in the first few days of the Somme campaign. By September, the RFC had sustained 100 per cent casualties in 18 weeks and experienced squadron commanders were temporarily forbidden to fly in an attempt to preserve at least some basic fighting structure. Battle hardened survivors made a point of not acknowledging the arrival of new recruits, certain in the knowledge they would not be around very long. If they did not get close enough to anyone to like them, they need not mourn their deaths. Seemingly immune to such losses, the point was reached when Trenchard's behaviour began to cause open concern at home. Noel Pemberton-Billing, an ex RNAS pilot and now an MP, publicly accused Britain of murdering gallant young officers, calling them "Fokker fodder" while Sykes, recently forgiven and reinstated in the War Office, was happy in private to damn Trenchard's tunnel vision. The nearest Trenchard came to admitting a problem of morale came in a letter to Sefton Brancker, ex fellow commander of No. 3 Wing and now Director of Organisation at the War Office. "I am afraid some of the pilots are getting a bit rattled," he conceded. Even so, though many privately considered Trenchard insensitive to casualty lists, few of the junior commanders under Trenchard had the temerity to object. One squadron leader to show both the courage and the compassion to ask that his men of the 60th Squadron, who, in a matter of weeks had suffered 50 per cent losses, the survival of any individual pilot averaging three weeks, should be rested. His name was Dowding, Hugh Caswall Tremenheere "Stuffy" Dowding, scathingly referred to by Trenchard as "that dismal Jimmy" given to "pernickety primness". With bad grace, Trenchard acceded to Dowding's request, promptly labelling him as weak and arranging his immediate posting to a training brigade back in Britain. With the defence of Britain in 1940 in mind, it is perhaps fortunate that Trenchard did not have Dowding shot for cowardice.

It is unlikely that Trenchard would have been permitted to campaign in the manner he did had he been German or French. Just as, when still a junior officer, he had considered he must have been making progress if he had earned the heartfelt antipathy of his brother officers, so he came to an equally perverse logical conclusion that the longer the casualty lists, the better the RFC must be performing. If the Germans were losing fewer men and machines, this only demonstrated their inferiority and lack of fighting spirit. It must be said that he was aided in this by the attitude to war of his pilots. In the early years of the war, the aircrew were drawn exclusively from the middle and upper class ranks of rugby playing, public school boys, entry into the élite facilitated if you could ride a horse and sail a boat. They alone, apparently, could be depended upon for that fighting spirit and power of leadership required to take the fight to the Germans. Who else, when the sand of the desert was sodden red, the Gatling jammed and the Colonel dead, could rally the ranks with the cry of "play up, play up and play the game"? Until late 1917, when crippling losses demanded it, both Henderson and Trenchard resisted all suggestions that pilots should be recruited from amongst the ranks of non-commissioned officers on the grounds that they would not have the correct sense of duty. Up until that time, it had frequently been more difficult to obtain a trained fitter or rigger than a bright eyed volunteer pilot. Certainly, when obliged in the closing stages of the war to train NCOs and also recruit extensively from the Dominions, particularly Canada, war in the air changed from being a deadly sport to a deadly business. Chivalry died as the only good German became a dead German, even if this occasionally involved the despatch of an enemy hanging defenceless from a parachute. No longer were wreaths dropped over enemy lines at the loss of a respected foe.

But the die was already struck. The whole ethos of the future British air force had already been established in those early years of its tragic yet joyous birth. Manfred von Richthofen, the Red Baron, who likened French attacking spirit to "bottled lemonade, lacking tenacity," commented that "Englishmen see in flying nothing but sport." He, like many of his colleagues, could not understand the English compulsion to shoot at anything that moved. Though obliged at times to do so, to the British strafing a plane on the ground was akin to shooting a sitting bird. In similar fashion, whereas German pilots, having successfully accomplished a bombing mission, would make every attempt to get home safely, British pilots would feel compelled to fight even when facing hopelessly overwhelming odds from a tactically unfavourable position in terms of height and sun. The German attitude of "he who fights and runs away, lives to fight another day" was anathema to Trenchard but also mistakenly seen as pure funk by British pilots. It was a madcap bravery of which their commanders took full advantage. Trenchard, even Henderson, opposed the use of parachutes, presumably to discourage the pilot from jumping while there was still some fight left in the plane. As a result, Richthofen recorded that over half of his victims burned to death, trapped in their blazing machines.

Trenchard also assiduously set his mind against the use of fighter escorts for his bombers, considering the aeroplane as no defence against the aeroplane. Though fighter versions of the DH2 and FE2 would occasionally escort the virtually defenceless reconnaissance planes, fighters he dismissed as purely glamorous and of no fighting consequence. Bombers would "always get through". As early as October 1915, the Germans had begun sending fighters against the British bombers but Trenchard's only reaction was to advise special training of bomber crews to combat them. As a result, Trenchard, with his obsolete BE2s, had temporarily lost control of his sector of the front to the new Fokkers. The BE2, minus its observer in order to carry more bombs, had no means by which it could fight its way home; any meeting with a Fokker a death sentence. Nothing had changed from the days when, as a boy, Trenchard had shown a marked disinclination to learn from anyone or anything. In spite of such an early lesson on how vulnerable to fighters bombers were by day, the bomber, he strenuously maintained, must be able to fight its own way out of trouble, a deluded conviction of a man who, brave though he undoubtedly was, never flew operationally himself to learn at first hand. It was a pig-headed notion that was destined in future years to become fatal dogma.

As to the aircraft, overall it would be difficult to argue that one side had an advantage over the other. During the conflict's closing months, Britain, who had begun so far behind both France and Germany, possessed the most powerful airforce in the world, producing between January and October 1918 over 27,000 aircraft. The Royal Flying Corps, numbering some 2,000 souls in 1914, had become the Royal Air Force of nearly 300,000 in 1918. Throughout the war, however, aerial supremacy, whether locally over a Wing's sector or generally over the whole Front, fluctuated. Factors governing this balance of power were many; morale, misguided tactics, inadequate training, irregular supplies; but, more often than not, it could be traced to the introduction on one side or the other of a particularly successful machine. The excellent German series of Albatross fighters accounted for their almost total supremacy in the autumn of 1916, certainly for "Bloody April" of 1917 when the RFC lost 30 per cent of its strength. At the other extreme, the British RE8s, made in vast numbers, were heartily disliked by their pilots, despite Trenchard's efforts to reassure them by arriving in one for squadron inspections.

Individual pilots had their favourites, whatever their virtues or vices. The SE5s, the Bristol F2Bs, the Sopwith Camels and One and a Half Strutters; all had their protagonists. The "aces" were usually associated with a particular plane; Rittmeister Manfred Freiherr von Richthofen, son of a Silesian nobleman, the aristocratic hunter, and his red Fokker or, later, Albatross; the withdrawn, one eyed, merciless Mick Mannock, son of a working class family, and his SE5. Boelke, the deep thinking tactician, and Immelmann, the innovator, with their Fokkers; the loner Albert Ball, killed in his SE5 before he was 21, and the Canadian, Billy Bishop, in his Nieuport Scout. But all the aces of the day were fighter pilots, their prowess graded according to their number of "kills". It followed that the planes they flew were those read about in the newspapers. The bomber ace and his number of missions flown would have to wait for the next war and arguably the finest aircraft flown by the British during World War 1, the DH4, was a bomber and thereby less likely to reach the headlines. But, had you asked the pilots who flew them, like Squadron Commander Wilfrid Freeman, survivor of the early weeks of war, they would have told you the DH4, de Havilland's first tractor plane, was way ahead of its time.

First flown by de Havilland himself at Hendon in August 1916, it was an instant success. The first squadrons began to appear in France in March 1917, flying their first offensive sorties over Valenciennes in April. The RNAS also knew a good plane when they saw one and acquired the DH4 for their strategic bombing. The Americans were impressed. They would ultimately build 4,800 of the 6,200 flown, using them for civilian purposes long after the war. Lindbergh would fly one. Powered with a Rolls Royce or more powerful Liberty 12 engine, it would carry 500 lbs of bombs up to 23,500 feet for nearly seven hours. But the feature that enamoured it to its crew was its speed - 143 miles per hour. Pitiful in an age of supersonic flight and space travel but, in its day, supreme; faster than any contemporary fighter on either side; for a lengthy period the fastest plane in the world, almost immune to interception.

It is unlikely that de Havilland designed his plane according to the concept that speed was the best form of defence; it simply happened to turn out that way. But de Havilland possessed one vital gift, the ability to learn from experience. He was not too proud to listen. He took every opportunity to fly to France to benefit from accounts given by those who flew the DH4 in action. He took account of their concern about some slight tail flutter. He had been accustomed to doing this in the days of Sykes and the BE2s and DH2s. Now he developed a rapport with Wilfrid Freeman, a wise, wily Presbyterian Scot, a relationship of unforseen consequence. Heavily armed as the DH4 was with two Vickers and one or two Lewis machine guns, fitted out in the classical defensive mode of the time, it was no better equipped to fight its way out of trouble than the next bomber. But, in its speed, pilots began to find their best defence. They began to realise that the faster they flew, the safer they were. However, who, with Trenchard in command, would have even contemplated suggesting to him that, if they were to throw overboard all four machine guns and all their ammunition, even speedier flight from the target, eschewing all unnecessary combat, would provide even more secure defence?

Brancker, back at the War Office, must be credited with the vision that led to the DH4's success. The Royal Aircraft Factory at Farnborough still held the whiphand in military aircraft production and the large order that went to Airco only went through with his backing. Several production lines, including BE2s at Farnborough, had to be curtailed, so impressed had Brancker been with the accuracy of the DH4, with its gyroscopic bomb sight and automatic direction finder for the pilot. Almost predictably, Trenchard was not so impressed, stating in a letter to de Havilland, after damning the plane with faint praise, "... but I do not think it is entirely suitable for bomb dropping." Such an attitude from the General Officer Commanding, plus, perversely, that most precious asset, its speed, combined to blunt its impact. They resulted in a considerable proportion of the production being diverted into fighter and reconnaissance versions when perfectly adequate Bristols and Sopwiths already existed. But their capabilities as bombers was not to be ignored and, in October 1917, when an élite bombing force, under Lt Colonel Cyril Newall, was formed with a view to truly strategic bombing and to break the stranglehold on bombing policy held by Trenchard, it was the DH4 that was chosen. But the first long-range daylight bombing attack by Newall's élite force on Saarbrücken was only one outcome of another battle, a political struggle at the centre of which those three soldiers, Henderson, Sykes and Trenchard, were once more drawn together; Henderson with reluctance, Trenchard with disgust. And Sykes? He probably rather enjoyed it.

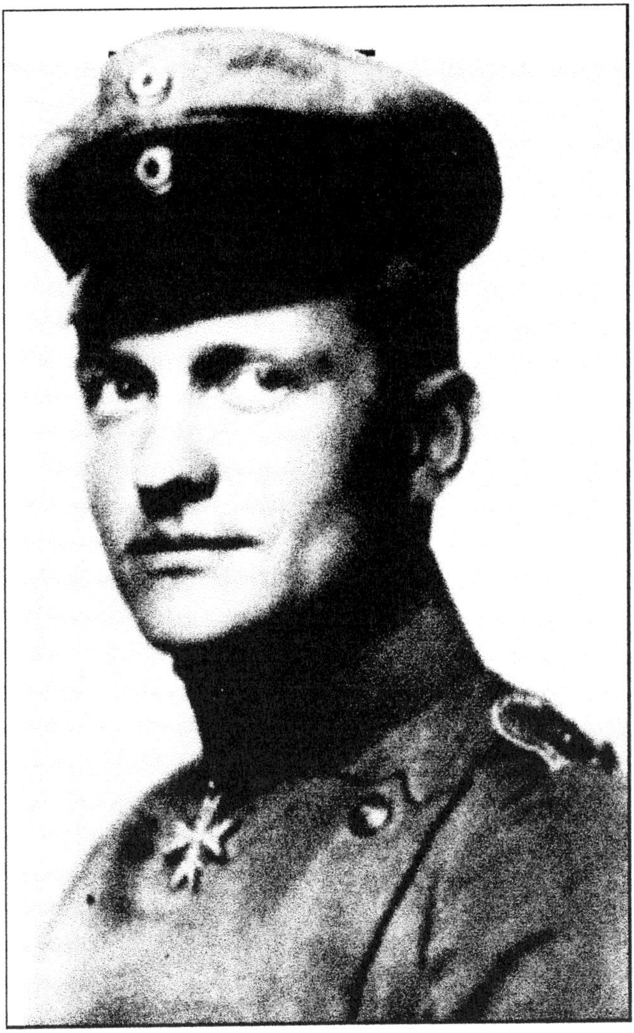

Chapter Four

As regards political influence over the RFC, it was negligible up until mid-1915. If the air force commanders had gone to war with no previous experience to guide them as they struggled with the steepness of the learning curve, their political masters could hardly have been expected to cope any better. Asquith's War Cabinet and the War Office were quite happy to accept that the most effective use of the new fangled machines was best left to the field commanders with no political implications other than the need to adjudicate in the constant bickering between the Navy and the Army. Few politicians, Churchill apart, had any conception of the potential for destruction these frail wood and wire contraptions possessed. If the field commanders insisted that they were needed for the effective prosecution of modern warfare, together with training of sufficient volunteers foolish enough to want to fly them, then it was the Government's duty to provide them, nothing more. There their responsibility rested and it was only understandable then that they should turn to their own factory at Farnborough to manufacture them. Private enterprise had little chance in competition, their only hope being to obtain licences, permitting them to build planes designed at the Royal Aircraft Factory. With such a monopoly in effect, it was fortunate for the RFC that de Havilland's FE2 and the BE2, particularly, held their own in the air for as long as they did.

What began to concentrate the politicians' minds was the death of five Londoners at the hands of Hauptmann Linnarz in the early hours of June 1, 1915. Bombs dropped previously by both Zeppelins and aircraft on targets as widespread as Yarmouth, Colchester, Faversham and Ramsgate had made the newspapers but little more. But Linnarz's bombs had struck at the very heart of Empire; too close for political comfort. Even so, the politicians rode the minor storm of letters to the Press and questions in the

House. Henderson, the only senior officer with any real experience of what was going on in the air, was brought home to the War Office to give his advice and they were fortunate in that the Zeppelin threat did not assume the proportions feared. During the whole of 1915, no more than 170 civilians were to be killed and 450 wounded as a result of enemy air action, a mere afternoon's skirmish in terms of the Western Front.

Churchill, singled out to be made the scapegoat for the Dardanelles fiasco, resigned from the Government, choosing to look for excitement in France with the 6th Royal Scots Fusiliers, Trenchard's old regiment, while Henderson was drawn inexorably into the political infighting at home. With Kitchener's influence on the wane, Henderson was given a permanent seat on the War Council where he spent most of his time quelling what he saw as damaging rivalry between the Army and the Navy as they fought over limited resources. It was an experience that confirmed in him the belief that there was only one logical solution, the creation of an air force independent of both the Army and Navy with a Council and Ministry of its own. It became a cause to which he would apply his considerable ability, becoming the seminal influence to which others later would lay parental claim.

Sykes also was on his way back. In March 1916, he was nominally on the strength of the 4th Mounted Division at Colchester as Quartermaster General. Within a month, he had acquired a rather nebulous posting to the War Office as Deputy General of Organisation, watching and waiting in the wings.

In May, in a half-hearted attempt to establish some sort of aeronautical hierarchy in place of a Joint War Air Committee which had lasted but two months, a new Air Board was formed with Lord Curzon as President. Curzon, at one time the youngest Viceroy of India, had no cause to love the military. It had been a head to head clash with his Commander in Chief of the Indian Army, Kitchener, that had brought about Curzon's resignation from all the pomp and prestige of the vice-regency, something he was not likely to forgive. And now he had as his most senior military commander that Kitchener clone, Trenchard, who had no intention of taking orders from some jumped-up politician he described as "that mountain of conceit and power seeking pedant". It might have been true that, on this occasion, Trenchard had a point, in that Curzon was everything Trenchard despised, but it did nothing to underpin any vestige of political control that might exist over the RFC in France. This was now virtually under Trenchard's supreme command. How the RFC was employed in France would be decided by Trenchard and his only master, Haig.

In June 1916, Churchill was back as an MP and Henderson sacked O'Gorman, relaxing the Royal Aircraft Factory's iron grip on aircraft production, freeing firms like Airco to follow their own stars. In July, David Lloyd-George, previously the Minister for Munitions, was appointed Secretary of State for War to replace Kitchener who now lay at the bottom of the North Sea but had for years been no more than a figurehead. The political backbone was stiffening as the struggle on the Somme began. One of Lloyd-George's early tasks was to announce that, with a total of 35 destroyed, due principally to improved planes, guns and ammunition, the Zeppelin threat was effectively over. As the Somme offensive ran its bloody course to its inconclusive end, leaving the country to count the cost in young men's lives, and all remained quiet on the Home Front, minds, both military and political, were overcome with an awful, weary inertia. Lloyd-George, though nominally Secretary of State for War, was constantly frustrated in that most of the decisions of importance were made at the War Office by a soldier, Sir William Robertson, the Chief of the Imperial General Staff. On December 1, unable any longer to bear what he saw as an intellectual vacuum within which the whole war effort was being waged, he resigned from the Government, forcing Asquith, languid from years spent in high society and hounded by the Press following costly failure on the Somme, to resign also as Prime Minister. On the December 7, 1916, David Lloyd-George, no great admirer of the military mind, became Prime Minister.

One of Lloyd-George's first moves was to form a small War Cabinet of five members to replace the previous twenty three. Two appointments to this Cabinet, which would sit permanently, were hardly designed to enthral Trenchard. One was Curzon, the other Lord Milner. A passionate imperialist, Milner had been High Commissioner in southern Africa and Governor of Cape Colony and, with his intransigent belief in the supremacy of British military might, was held by many to be at least partially responsible for the outbreak of the Boer War. His autocratic attitude also ensured his methods of resettling the Boers after the war failed. Trenchard would surely have formed his own opinion of him from his days in South Africa. There was however one glimmer of hope. When Minister of Munitions, Lloyd-George had realised that static trench warfare would be won ultimately, not by the brilliance of any individual commander, but by the side with the greater resources. His highly effective if controversial methods had ensured sufficient supplies for the Somme campaign, daring to antagonise his civil servants by recruiting the best brains from private industry to spur the munitions factories. His appointment therefore of William Weir, a technical expert, to control all aeronautical supplies came as no surprise; and Weir, a deceptively diffident man, was a strong advocate of the bomber; his dream, mass raids on German industry. The supply of DH4 squadrons to France, begun in March, was assured. The controversy over how they should be employed was yet to arise.

The Zeppelin campaign of terror was over, any slight damage to morale or material failing to justify the losses now being sustained against a belatedly organised defence against the lumbering, vulnerable craft. The German Army would dispense with their services completely though their Navy still found uses for them. That did not mean that the Germans would not try again, this time with aircraft. Operation Turk's Cross was planned to involve the Gotha bombers with their 78-foot wing span and the giant four-engined Staaken R VIs and their two-ton bomb loads; the Lancasters of WW1. On June 13, 1917, London took its first blows. In broad daylight, 14 German planes dropped over 100 bombs, killing 162 and injuring 432, without loss to themselves. This time the civil population's fear and fury, backed by that of Parliament, was not to be denied.

Pemberton-Billing, MP, now known as "the Member for Air", became the first to openly demand the indiscriminate retaliatory bombing of civilians. Public hysteria was such as to demand reprisals against captured U-boat crews, pressure to which the Admiralty bowed, despite a personal plea from King George, until the Germans returned tit for tat. It was a time for cool heads.

A two-man committee was immediately set up at the very highest level; Lloyd-George himself and Jan Christiaan Smuts, scientist, lawyer and one of the most brilliant intellects of his day. Their brief was to study Home Defence. But this was not enough. What the populace demanded was retribution and Smuts recommended the formation of an independent bomber force to take the war to Germany, a suggestion strongly supported by both

Henderson and Sykes. The Smuts report was the first British official acceptance of the premise that wars could be won without land battles but fell short of defining precise targets. Trenchard, however, summoned to a special meeting of the War Cabinet, turned stubborn, this time with some degree of reason on his side. Such an offensive action would have been very much to his liking but, determined not to be diverted from his support of Haig at the Front, he argued that it was pointless to undertake any retaliatory terror campaign unless they were prepared to go all the way and they did not have the resources to do that.

Public outcry reached its climax in July when thousands watched as over 40 Gotha bombers circled over London at 3,000 feet, resulting in the House of Commons going into secret session to debate what should be done. The only apparent outcome was the appointment of Churchill as Minister of Munitions while Weir sent a specification to Handley Page for a giant four engined bomber of their own, the V1500, designed to match the Gotha and bomb Berlin. But there was to be no airborne holocaust. The initial Gotha raids lost impetus and, by late summer, crippling losses in daylight soon forced them to change to night attacks. Of the 92 Gothas that took off on the last daylight raids, such was the defence that only 55 reached Britain, a mere 20 fought through to London of which 13 were lost. Sporadic raids on Britain would continue, both by day and by night, until May 1918 when, finally convinced that British morale was not going to crack, the Germans shifted their bomber sorties to where they were more urgently needed, back on the Western Front.

But the debate had now been opened. What was this thing, the bomber, that the inventors had presented to them, the men of power. How was it to be put to best effect? That it could cause considerable destruction was not in doubt. But, whether dropped on trenches, lines of communication, supply depots or even on manufacturing bases back within Germany, its bomb was no diffcrent from a shell fired from a gun. In fact, at that time the destructive power of a bomber fell a long way short of that of a gun. It would later be estimated that it took two whole bomber squadrons to equal the destructive power of just one 155 mm gun, three long distance bomber squadrons that of five 75 mm guns. But the bomber carried a far more deadly load, terror; fear and dread that could be aimed at a man's very soul. To what extent would this be effective? Moreover, was it a morally acceptable weapon of war?

Smuts, in his first report, had visions of what the future might hold. "... the day may not be far off when aerial operations, with their devastation of enemy lands and destruction of industrial and populace centres on a vast scale, may become the principal operations of war ..." Trenchard fully agreed. After all, it was no more than the ultimate expression of an inflexibly offensive dogma. In a memo to the War Cabinet, he accepted the premise that the enemy's morale could be undermined by relentless bombing, including targets no more specific than "large cities", this at a time when the bomber was finding difficulty in hitting a target the size of a small town. Nevertheless, he maintained his opposition to such planning, including the formation of an air force divorced from the Army, on the grounds that the diversion of resources required would undermine the chances of victory where he was convinced it would still be won, on the Western Front.

Churchill was not so convinced. "It is improbable," he wrote, "that any terrorisation of the civil population which could be achieved by air attack would compel the Government of a nation to surrender." Civilian casualties he saw as inevitable but not the primary objective. Having witnessed the Londoners' reaction to the

Gotha raids, he thought that bombing might even strengthen a country's resolve.

It was a time for radical rethinking. Trenchard had formed what he referred to as his Distant Offensive Patrols but, unlike both the French and the Germans, spread their efforts so widely in obsolescent machines as to incur heavy losses; 40 per cent casualties on patrols during the Battle of Cambrai. The crunch came when Naval 10 Squadron, temporarily under his command because of such losses and ordered to repeat a bombing raid they had not carried out to Trenchard's satisfaction previously, refused, saying they were "not for it" and had to be taken out of the line and returned to Dunkirk. The result was the formation, without reference to Trenchard, of a special Wing, comprised of two flights of DH4s, an élite force under the command of Lt Colonel Cyril Newall, their sole function to bomb the Saar-Lorraine region. Smuts and Henderson were beginning to feel their feet, two intellectuals growing in their confidence that the Prime Minister would back them against the military establishment. The crucial moment came in October 1917 when, in a written memo to the Chief of the Imperial General Staff, Henderson strongly recommended the merging of the RFC and the RNAS into one force, distinct from the two great services. The immediate result was his expulsion from the Army Council by a vindictive Army high command and his removal from the post of Director General of the Directorate of Military Aeronautics. This simply played into Henderson's hands, allowing more time for him to convince Smuts he was right. With Smuts converted, it was but a short step to Lloyd-George. Within a month, the text of the Air Force Bill was published in *The Times*, with a clear commitment to establish an Air Council and Secretary of State for Air, the Council to be of equal standing with the Army Council and Admiralty. On November 29, the Air Force Bill became law, the whole process having taken no more than weeks once the nettle had been grasped. On the January 3, 1918, the Air Council was formed by an Order in Council. Henderson had won.

And Sykes? He was now to be found on the Supreme War Council in Versailles, cultivating the friendships of such men as Woodrow Wilson, President of the United States of America.

The new Air Council made strange bedfellows. Lord Rothermere, a shy but extremely astute and successful business man, was the first Secretary of State for Air at the Air Ministry. Henderson was made Vice President. William Weir, still advocating bigger and better bombers, was Minister of Munitions and Lloyd-George made Trenchard an offer he could not refuse. Knighted, reluctantly he became the first Chief of the Air Staff but not before he had left the RFC with a last memorandum stressing the offensive nature of aviation. It was already common knowledge that "Boom" Trenchard had little time for civilians; politicians, in particular, he was known to detest. In France, stubbornly driving his men and machines in support of his idol, he had been happy to ignore those back in the War Office in London and leave the dirty business of politics to others - setting aside for the moment his part in getting rid of Sykes. But now he was one of them. Inarticulate at best, he was now thrust unwillingly amongst those for whom he could hardly find a kind word. He was to experience at first hand, the machinations of men driven as much by the desire for electoral approval as by patriotism. It was a relationship doomed to failure.

Within three months, predictably, Trenchard had quarrelled with Rothermere who thought him "... of dull unimaginative mind". On April 1, 1918, the Royal Air Force was born and, within 11 days, Trenchard had resigned. Rothermere, equally disillusioned with political infighting, also resigned to be replaced as Secretary of State for Air by William Weir, now Lord Weir. Rothermere could return to his business interests but what was to be done with Trenchard? There were no grounds for replacing the very able John Salmond who had taken over from Trenchard as GOC in France. Salmond, a born communicator, always ready to listen, was already earning his reputation as "a pilot's general". To replace him again with a man who had a reputation for being unconcerned by casualty lists would have had incalculable results. So Trenchard was assigned to Special Duties at HQ in France where he must have been a constant thorn in Salmond's flesh.

And Sykes? He, now Major General Sir Frederick Sykes, returned from Versailles to take over as Chief of the Air Staff, senior to Trenchard once more. This led to another resignation, Henderson's, as he "earnestly desired to escape from the atmosphere of falsehood and intrigue which has enveloped the Air Ministry." It virtually marked the end of a distinguished career.

It left Lloyd-Goerge with a loose cannon, Trenchard. How was he to be tied down? The solution was to give Trenchard a small force of his own; 49 heavy night bombers, 75 day bombers and 16 fighters. It would be called the Independent Air Force or 8th Brigade, its function to hit German industrial targets, primarily chemical, iron and steel, and to concentrate on one town until morale broke. Once more, Trenchard agreed to a command on one proviso, that he would accept no orders from Sykes, only from Weir. Weir, agreeing, left Trenchard in little doubt as to his own bombing philosophy. Writing to Trenchard, he said, "I would not be too exacting in regards accuracy bombing railway stations in the middle of towns. The Germans are susceptible to bloodiness and I would not mind a few accidents due to inaccuracy." In return he received no objection from Trenchard who replied, "... the moral effect of bombing stands undoubtedly to the material in proportion of 20 to 1." There was a later exchange of letters. "I would very much like," Weir wrote, "if you would start up a really big fire in one of the German towns," going on to explain how the older, built up areas were more likely to burn well, with their mainly wooden construction, than the more modern buildings. "I do not think you need be anxious about our degree of accuracy," Trenchard replied. "All the pilots drops their eggs well into the middle of the town generally."

As it transpired, Trenchard ignored Weir also, taking orders from no one, using the IAF as a private concern, dismissing complaints from Sykes that the Force was not being used as intended, viewing as simply a lack of trust, reasonable requests from Lord Milner, the War Secretary, that the War Cabinet be kept better informed. In practice, Trenchard's continued unfailing loyalty to Haig diverted a great deal of his effectiveness away from strategic raids. Despite the DH4 proving its ability in attack, bombing Cologne from 14,000 feet in daylight, his strategic attacks, depleted by planes occupied elsewhere in a tactical role, were weak and widely dispersed, lacking the concentrated maximum effort found so effective by the French. Resulting losses from fighter attacks on long haul missions mounted to the point when one or other operations had, at least temporarily, to cease. Faced with the choice, Trenchard's strategic bombing dwindled, becoming negligible and, finding his force becoming ineffective in both operational modes, he was prompted to write in his diary, "A more gigantic waste of effort and personnel there has never been in any war." The Force, designed by politicians for strategic purposes, had been nullified by a soldier with a tactically gridlocked mind.

It was strange then that this Force which, in the opinion of its own commander, was "a gigantic waste of effort and personnel", should be replaced in the last few months of the war by an even larger one, the Inter-Allied Independent Air Force. Even stranger than that, though the French had achieved far greater success in strategic bombing than the British and Billy Mitchell, the US commander of a formidable combined French and American bomber force was already carrying out mass raids in the Meuse-Argonne campaign, involving over 200 planes at a time, Trenchard should be given the overall command, having once publicly stated that under no circumstances would he co-operate with the French. It was but another measure of the stature of the man in other men's minds.

Such was the mystique, the aura of infallibility that this honest but inflexibly stupid man had developed. The Inter-Allied IAF was formed too late in the war for Trenchard's control to show any effect; the war ended before it could be fully co-ordinated. But Trenchard had already laid down the rules by which the RAF's bomber force would always play the game. Relentless frontal attacks on a wide front, total disregard for the odds, the spurning of all assistance from fighters, those were to be the only paths to victory. He would say repeatedly at briefings, "If I knew for a fact that this raid would shorten the war by one day, you'd go and be glad you were going," spoken in tones that implied he envied them the privilege - and probably did. After just such an attempted daylight raid by 99 Squadron on Mainz, of the entire squadron only two planes returned. And Trenchard's reaction? "They had a great fight," he reported to Weir. "I went round at once and told them that as long as they kept up their spirits, it was a victory for us. This, I said is what defeats the Hun so much ..."

As late as July 1918, a few months only away from his greatest challenge, how to come to terms with peace, Trenchard still showed no hint of compromise. Speaking to young, inexperienced replacement pilots of the IAF who listened, starry-eyed with pride, he reminded them that, if sending them all at once across the lines, never to return, would shorten the war by one week, it would be his duty to send them. He also remarked that while, unfortunately, he was condemned to drive around in a Rolls Royce and sit in an easy chair, he had never thought any deed of sacrifice and devotion too great for their powers.

Chilling words indeed, not only for those in his audience soon to die but also for another later generation for whom they would assume almost biblical significance. It has been said that all wars commence on the basis of the previous one. If this was true, the next war's strategic bombing campaign would begin with massed daylight, unescorted formations, brushing aside futile attempts at air defence, ostensibly to attack military targets but happy if, in so doing, the heart of some enemy city was burned to the ground. It would remain to be seen if this would prove to be true.

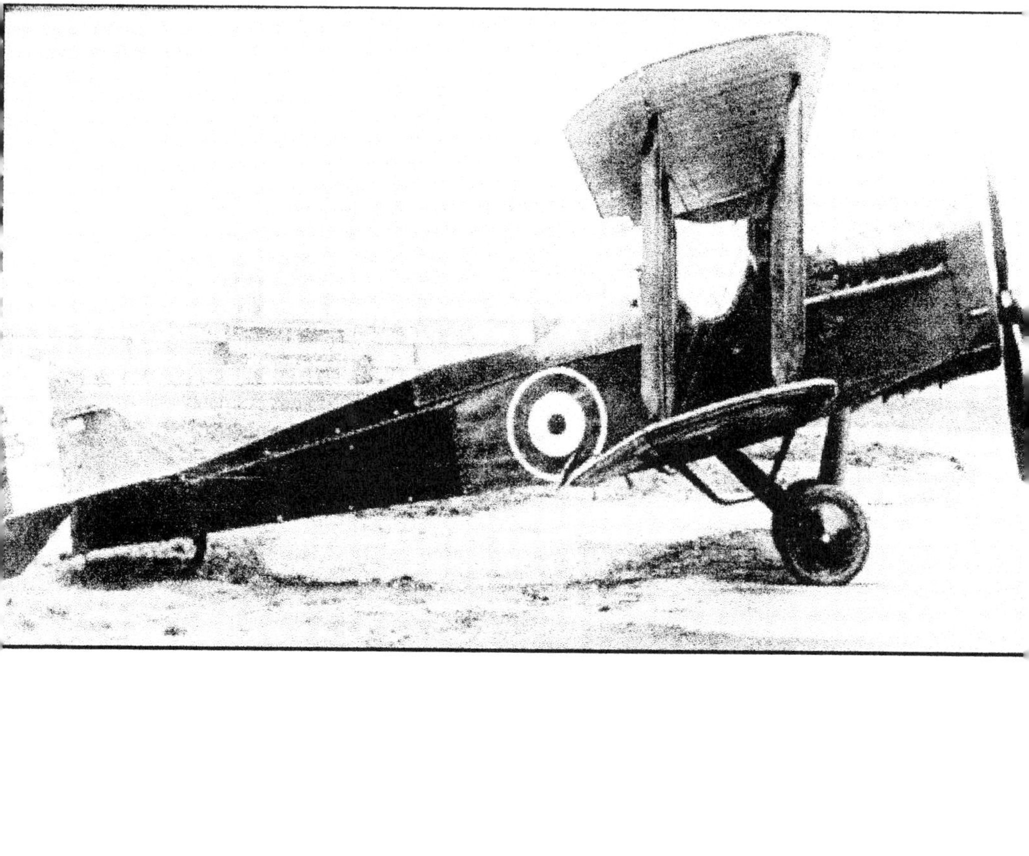

Chapter Five

The Armistice signed, it was unlikely that Trenchard, ordered with the rest to lay down his arms, would do so without some final gesture of defiance. Since his return to France, his instructions to take the war to the German civilians, though thoroughly approved by him in principle, had been largely ignored as his deeply held loyalty to the Army had made its demands. It had been tacitly understood that he, as commander of an independent force, could never take advice, let alone orders, from Salmond, previously junior to him, then the officer commanding the RAF in France. But Trenchard's final action in France was as typical of the man as it was infuriating to Salmond. On hearing of the ceasefire, Trenchard telegraphed Marshal Foch, Allied C in C in France, requesting permission to return the Independent Air Force to Haig. They may have changed the colour of his uniform, the design of his buttons and badges, but the man inside was still a soldier, prepared to surrender his sword only to another soldier. This was the man later to be described as the Father of the Royal Air Force.

A fighter without a fight, Trenchard returned home, demanding to be put on half pay, a demand refused by Weir. This proved fortunate for Trenchard's peculiar qualities were soon to be put to good use. In January 1919, Churchill, now Secretary of State for War and Air, ordered him to Southampton docks where hundreds of discontented troops, resentful at being returned to France, were bordering on full blown mutiny. By singling out the ring leaders, then bringing to bear the full power of his reputation and formidable personality, not to mention his towering physical presence, in a fearless eyeball to eyeball confrontation, Trenchard subdued the tentative mutineers and sent them on their way.

It was a minor event in itself but was destined to have unexpectedly major long-term consequences. Lloyd-George was anxious to wind up the Air Ministry, to return to the two service system of old. Churchill, strongly influenced by Weir who, though now a business man again was still politically active, was fighting to maintain the RAF as an independent service. He needed all the help he could get and Weir convinced him that Trenchard's one-eyed stubbornness, so controversial in war, might be just the quality needed in peace. The showdown in Southampton docks tipped the scales. Churchill sent for Trenchard and offered him the position of Chief of Staff once more. But, Trenchard pointed out, Major General Sykes already occupied that post.

Sykes was at the Versailles Peace Conference, leading the British Air Section, basking in the heady atmosphere surrounding the likes of Wilson, the liberal, Clemenceau, the draconian, and Lloyd-George the mercurial. Inspired by such grandeur, he strongly advocated a peacetime independent air force of 62 service and 92 cadre squadrons together with a further 37 Dominion cadre squadrons. Such grandiose plans did nothing to appease the Army and the Navy or make Churchill's task any easier. Trenchard's proposals for a slimmer, purely offensive force suited Churchill and Sykes came home from Versailles to a bombshell. While all the formalities were observed, he was "encouraged" to resign as CAS and to assume a new post with the grand title of Controller-General of Civil Aviation. He would still work within the Air Ministry but as a civilian. Trenchard, yet again, had prevailed over his old rival. Sykes would go on to other things. He would produce the Civil Flying Regulations, plan the Empire air routes. He would become an MP, a Privy Councillor, a Governor of Bombay. But his service career, which had started so brightly and in which he had achieved high office, had always been overshadowed by the predatory presence of Trenchard. And Trenchard would show no mercy. When informed later that Sykes was to marry Isabel, daughter of the future Prime Minister, Bonar Law, Trenchard's only response was to suggest the only conclusion to be drawn was that Megan Lloyd-George must have refused him.

1919 was a time for retrospection and honest appraisal, stripped of the veil of wartime propaganda. In January, *The Times* gave the British losses due to enemy air raids between 1915 and 1918 as 498 civilian and 58 soldiers killed and 1913 injured; trivial figures in terms of wars to come and more the cause of anger and strengthened national resolve than terror and shattered morale. They paled into insignificance when compared with the 150,000 British citizens to die of influenza that winter.

Access on the ground was now possible to enemy targets bombed by the British and a survey of the prolonged RNAS raids on the Saar blast furnaces failed to reveal any effect on local morale. The US Air Service bombing survey weighed in with its own criticism. "Lack of a predetermined program, carefully calculated to destroy by successive raids those industries most vital in maintaining Germany's fighting forces has been the bombing campaign's greatest failure."

What might have occurred had the war gone on another year is pure conjecture. The Super Handley Pages and the Vickers Vimy heavy bombers, designed to shuttle bomb German cities including Berlin and thereby totally unsuited for Army co-operation, would then have been available to Trenchard. Judging by his methods adopted with the DH4s, when he could be persuaded by Salmond to divert them from aiding Haig, and his strategic bombing policy agreed with Weir with its mere lip service to industrial destruction, it is extremely unlikely that the US survey would have had cause to alter one word of its criticism. The tempo might have been raised but the theme would have been unchanged.

In June 1919, as the Treaty was being signed, four DH4s, in line ahead, flew over Versailles, a brave sight as, back in Britain, the bottom fell out of the aircraft manufacturing industry. At the time of the Armistice, the RAF had been the most powerful air force in the world with 96 squadrons in service. While there was no danger now of being shot out of the skies, fatal crashes were still commonplace but gone was the urgency to replace them. The Hun was vanquished. So, with no planes to design and build, what was to become of the likes of Captain Geoffrey de Havilland and O'Gorman, the Royal Aircraft Factory reject who had joined him once more at Airco?

There was no doubt that the DH4 had been de Havilland's supreme contribution to the conflict. Still being constructed in the USA, it was destined yet for a long and distinguished career. But de Havilland had not rested on his laurels. Further designs had followed. These, designed and built to restrictive official specifications, often progressing no further than the prototype stage, had culminated in the DH9. This bomber had shown great promise and much had been hoped of it. Sadly it had failed to live up to expectations but its limitations had not been discovered before it had been put into full-scale production. It had not been a total disaster and served the RAF for many years but perhaps the DH4 had set too high a standard. But whatever plane had been in production at the time, it would have felt the cold blast of a depressed market for military aircraft. Airco, Avro, Shorts, Sopwith, Bristol, Vickers; all would face a difficult time.

Trenchard, now firmly re-established as CAS, was soon into his stride. Convinced that the RAF's best chance of survival was in a lean, less financially demanding mode, within six months he had reduced the 96 squadrons to 23 of which only 10 were required to be serviceable at any one time. Assured of Churchill's support,

Trenchard was fortunate also in having under him an air force commander, John Salmond, with the generosity of spirit to put aside previous slights in the cause of independence. It was one thing, however, to demonstrate that they now had a small but efficient force, another to know what to do with it. Even in peacetime the Navy was required to "show the flag" as master of the seven seas. There was always some port in the far-flung empire that required the calming influence of a gunboat. India alone gave the Army its *raison d'être*. But what could be found for the RAF to do? Churchill did his best, declaring, "The first duty of the Royal Air Force is to garrison the British Empire." His words rang hollow as several Handley Pages crashed en route to India, described in the Rothermere Press as a "a trail of blood". But help was at hand, to arise from the unlikeliest of quarters. The "Mad Mullah" of Somaliland was to come to their aid, finding for the RAF a role that would ensure their future as an independent force.

It was a time when a tiny European offshore island ruled the greatest empire the world had ever known. British children would point proudly at their school atlases where up to a fifth of the land masses were coloured red. To gain possession of a foreign land, either by direct military conquest or as part of the spoils of war, was fairly straightforward; to maintain dominion over it considerably more difficult. From time to time, tiresome natives would rise up, impudently claiming the land to be theirs, rebelling against what Britain saw as law and order. They would need to be "taught a lesson". The Navy and the Army had their several methods. A gunboat would appear out of the mists to lob a few shells into the main square of some troublesome port. A raiding shore party would return aboard, leaving a few dead bodies to concentrate the survivors' minds. The Army would maintain a garrison in some god-forsaken corner of the world, manned by some homesick county regiment, from whence sporadic punitive patrols were launched, often to provide nothing more than fine sport for such inveterate warriors as the Pathans or the Mujahideen. Both methods had one thing in common, a constant drain on the Exchequer.

In 1920, British Somaliland was being particularly obdurate. The Mad Mullah, a militant fanatic with a gift for guerrilla warfare, was being acutely embarrassing to the Army who showed no sign of dealing with him. Trenchard despatched a squadron with clear instructions as to how they were to operate. There were no military targets as such; guerrilla fighters do not require vast industrial sites and have an aptitude for blending with the countryside. Small, defenceless towns and villages were reduced to rubble, the "civilian" population slaughtered. It need not be one of the Mullah's villages; any one would do as terror spread throughout the land to drive the Mullah from power. Peace was restored at a fraction of the price it would have cost the Army or the Navy to produce the same result.

The RAF had found its role, its brutal method of operating the first realisation of its true intention. Victory had been achieved without a shot being fired on the ground. Terror had been proved effective and, in the circumstances, cheap. Impressed at last, Curzon, the Foreign Secretary, Milner, the Colonial Secretary, and Churchill, Secretary of State for War, all three ardent imperialists, immediately ordered squadrons to be sent to far-flung outposts with instructions for "more of the same". To the North West Frontier of India went a Bristol Fighter Squadron. Its commander? Arthur Harris.

As if to celebrate the whole joyous affair, in July, at the age of 47, Trenchard married Mrs Katherine Boyle. The wedding took place in St Margaret's, Westminster. Maurice Baring was best man and Churchill spoke at the reception. It would come as no surprise that Lady Trenchard was soon pregnant.

They were momentous days for Geoffrey de Havilland also. Airco, near to collapse, sold out to BSA and, in September 1920, from the wreckage of a fine company, the de Havilland Aircraft Company arose. With financial help from Holt Thomas, always a staunch de Havilland supporter, a couple of DH18 fuselages were transported to a few huts at Stag Lane aerodrome in Edgeware. Of far greater potential were the men de Havilland took with him. Over some technical staff, recruited from Airco, Frank Hearle, ever faithful, would become Works Manager. Nixon would become Company Secretary and handle Finance, St Barbe Business and Sales. Charles Walker would be Chief of Aerodynamics and Stressing with Arthur Hagg, soon to be Head of Design, in charge of the Drawing Office. Frank Halford joined them from Farnborough as Chief Engine Designer. Their specialties varied but they all had certain qualities in common; they were young, keen and ambitious. What then did it matter if the only form of heating they had that first bitter winter was frequent games of football. Starting with a working capital of £1,875, somehow, they survived until, in 1921, they were joined by a dashing young pilot. Alan Cobham had a fine reputation dating back to his entry into the RFC in 1917. In years to come, Cobham's daring and endurance would put de Havilland's planes before the public gaze. What was more; he had "connections".

In 1921, as the de Havilland Aircraft Company struggled to find its first customers, David Henderson died. Though it is unlikely he would have succeeded without Weir's drive behind the scenes, Henderson was the true Father of the Royal Air Force, his claim to paternity usurped over the years by Trenchard. As Beaverbrook later observed of Trenchard, "He was a father who tried to strangle the infant at birth though he got the credit for the grown man." But the title has stuck. In fairness to Trenchard, he admitted that, "Henderson had twice the insight and imagination I had. It is doubtful whether the RAF or Britain realises its debt to him." Wherever justice lay between the claims to paternity, the fight for the infant's survival lay squarely on Trenchard's broad shoulders. Fortunately, during the early twenties, with Churchill now Colonial Secretary and Major Frederick Guest, a cousin of Churchill's, instated at the Air Ministry, he did not lack for staunch allies. As if to stake out their territory, Churchill, ever the visionary, declared, "We are sure that if, after a prolonged spell of peace, war on a grand scale suddenly broke out again, the Power which had made the most intensive study of aerial warfare would start with an enormous initial advantage, and the Power that neglected this form of active defence might well find itself fatally situated."

Brothers in arms, they all went off to the conference in Cairo where Britain and France were busily occupied carving up the Middle East between them. Part of the deals hammered out was that Britain "got" Iraq. It was here, in Iraq, that the principle of "active defence", a phrase that had tripped so lightly off Churchill's tongue, would find its final stamp of approval.

Before proving its worth in Iraq, there would be one last bitter battle at home. Beatty, the First Sea Lord, already depressed at the outcome of disarmament talks in Washington, launched his attack at a time of financial stringency as he saw the Navy's long respected role as the country's first line of defence, eroded, while Wilson, the CIGS, did all he could to block supplies to the RAF. Churchill once more intervened to rescue the RAF, reminding everyone that it had been created by an Act of Parliament. In March 1922, matters appeared to have been settled as Austen

Chamberlain, the Lord Privy Seal, made a statement in the House that the RAF was to be preserved. This marked a close run victory for Trenchard but only so long as a Coalition Government remained in power. In October, however, Lloyd-George resigned and Bonar Law, Frederick Sykes's father-in-law, became Prime Minister. Sykes had not long resigned as Controller of Civil Aviation in protest at the amount of money being spent on the RAF. A one time staunch protagonist of an independent air force, he had now convinced his father-in-law that control should return to the Army and Navy to the point that, when Law appointed Samuel Hoare as Secretary of State for Air, he warned him it would not be for long. Another Somaliland was required urgently. Iraq would provide it.

Churchill had decided, after the Cairo Conference, that the most suitable form of ruler for Iraq, from Britain's point of view that is, would be a king. Accordingly, on August 23, 1921, Emir Feisal had been crowned, protected by eight squadrons of Trenchard's RAF. The pattern of overseas control was emerging. In September 1922, an Anglo-Turkish crisis, the so called Chanak Incident, arose. The Turks had their eye on the oil rich northern province of Mosul. Kamel Pasha, the Turkish hero of Gallipoli, flexed his muscles, reoccupying Smyrna, massacring the Greeks in the process. Lloyd-George, pro-Greek, tried to rally support for military action against Kamel but found little or none amongst allies, Dominions or political colleagues. Even Churchill was in favour of placating Kamel. Few had the stomach for another major war so soon after the last. As Lloyd-George vacillated, Kamel drove on until faced with a British outpost in a neutral zone at a place called Chanak. The outpost had orders to stand firm and did so. There was a stand off from which Britain claimed victory. But Lloyd-George's popularity had been in decline and his dithering in dealing with the crisis was the final straw that brought him down.

The Trenchard Touch

On October 19, he resigned, days only after he had approved John Salmond's appointment as Air Officer Commanding HQ Iraq, the first air officer to command ground troops.

Salmond showed himself to be a brilliant commander in the field but, as Bonar Law proved to be as indecisive as Lloyd-George in dealing with incursions into Iraq by the Kurds under Sheik Mahmud, and as Guest was turning out to be a poor Secretary of State, Salmond's success owed much to Trenchard's unquestioning support at home. When Trenchard suggested that Salmond's air power could well be supplemented by fast armoured cars on the ground, Wilson, the CIGS, petulantly blocked all supplies. Unabashed, Trenchard converted some of his maintenance workshops and built his own. Rejoicing in Wilson's chagrin, vehicles, painted with RAF roundels and under Air Force command, were soon patrolling Iraq on the ground.

These Salmond put to good use together with the revolutionary practice of moving troops rapidly by air. But it was the bombing campaign that once again won the day. It was Somaliland all over again but on a much grander scale. In the face of some criticism of the bombing techniques in Somaliland, some of the "civilian" casualties were avoided as 24 hour warnings were occasionally given by leaflet. But the knowledge that to harbour or succour in any way rebel forces inevitably resulted in the loss of their homes, if not their lives, had a deeply demoralising effect that eventually overcame any patriotic or religious zeal. Terror once again had carried all before it, convincing Trenchard even further that, in a battle where civilian morale was the prime target, the enemy would always "squeal", as he put it, before the British.

By 1923, due to Salmond's brilliance and Trenchard's tenacity, the RAF was secure. They had even beaten the Royal Navy at Twickenham. Their existence still occasionally required justification as when Trenchard was required to appear before the Committee of Imperial Defence who sat as both judge and jury. But the RAF's accomplishments were already sufficient to see it through such irritating distractions from what was now uppermost in their thoughts. If they were to be the country's first line of defence, against whom would they most likely be actively defending? In 1923, the answer was quite clear - France.

Britain, in the disarmament process, had fallen well behind France who now had a commanding lead. The RAF's 12 squadrons for home defence compared unfavourably with France's 120. "With their proposed expansion by 1925," Trenchard warned, "the French could drop 325 tons in one day." To drive home the point further, he quoted Marshal Foch as saying, "... it is clear that such attack, owing to its crushing moral effect on a nation, may impress public opinion to the point of disarming the Government and thus become decisive." Terror, this time with a French accent.

In offering advice to his Government on defence, Trenchard's opinions were predictable. "It is on the bomber offensive that we must rely for defence. It is on the destruction of enemy industries and, above all, on the lowering of morale of enemy nationals caused by bombing that ultimate victory rests." By March 1924, the Air Staff was openly proclaiming its conversion to Trenchard's philosophy. In their Memorandum 11A, they stated their "... conviction that the correct approach is to bomb military objectives in populated areas to gain a decision from the effect on morale and the dislocation of civilian life."

As the distribution of airfields along the south coast was decided on the basis of France, rather than Germany, being the likely aggressor, so the Navy saw this once more as a slight to their traditional role. They had an ally in Rothermere, no friend of Trenchard, whose newspapers were only too happy to publish

Admiralty leaks in their continued campaign against the RAF. One such argument, made public, involved the vulnerability of capital ships to air attack. Trenchard held they had no real defence; Beatty claimed them to be indestructible from the air. The answer came from across the Atlantic. Mitchell, using DH4 bombers out of Langley Field, Virginia, attacked the old German battleship, *Ostfriesland*, and the cruiser, *Frankfurt,* sending them to the bottom within minutes.

It was a lesson to which both the US and Royal Navies found it convenient to turn a blind eye, with catastrophic consequences in later years at Pearl Harbour and off the coast of Malaya. But it proved a crucial triumph for the RAF in their battle with the Senior Service. Meanwhile, Bonar Law, dying of cancer, had gone, taking with him any last vestige of Sykes's influence. The Salisbury Committee on Strategy, comprised of Balfour, Weir and Peel, voted to expand the RAF. Trenchard could now sit on equal terms with the Army and the Navy on the newly formed Chiefs of Staff Committee. Sir Samuel Hoare, Secretary of State for Air, now a devoted Trenchard man under the welding influence of Ludlow-Hewitt, was granted Cabinet rank. The RAF's sense of security now bordered on that of arrogant superiority.

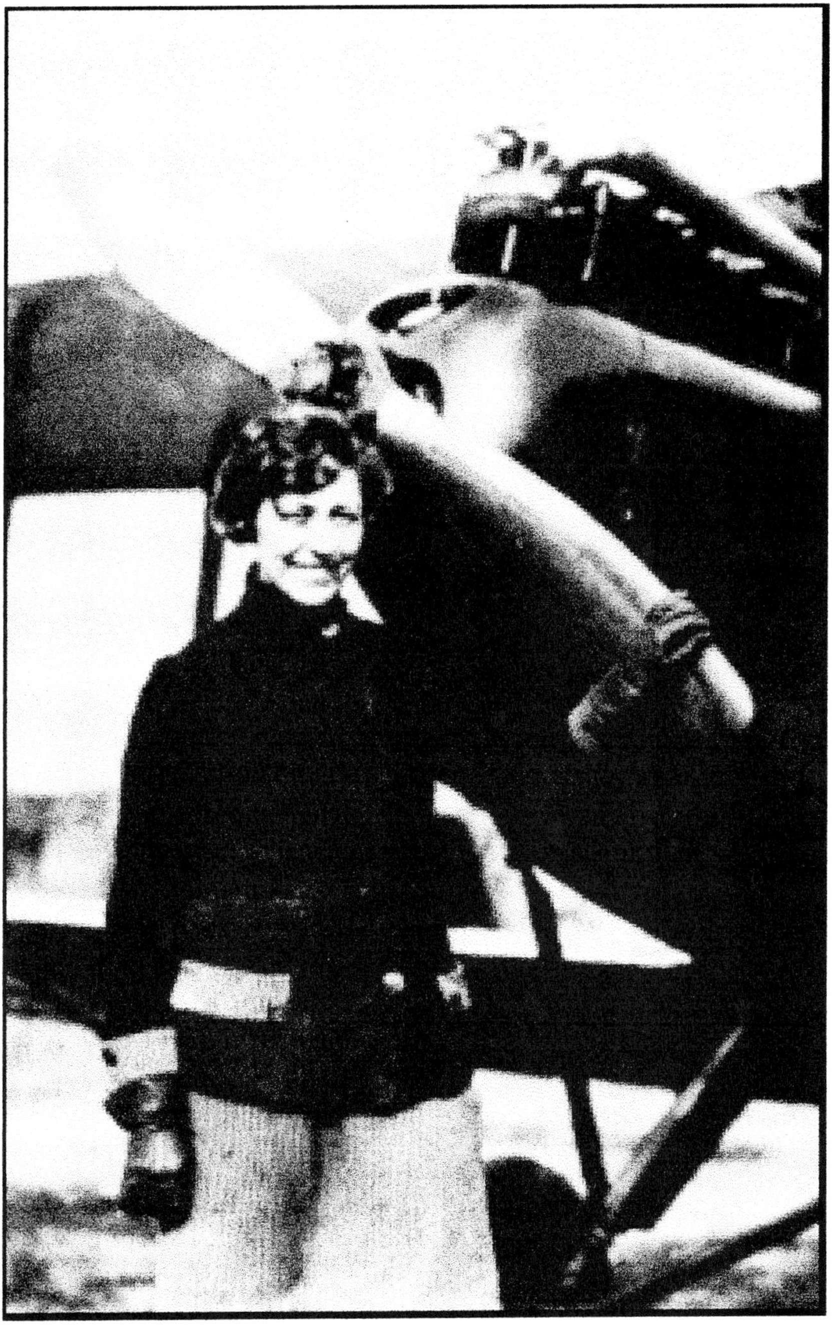

Chapter Six

If the late twenties and early thirties were times for the RAF, now safe from immediate extinction, to take breath, life in civil aviation was being lived with breath-taking excitement. Stag Lane had become increasingly busy, design after design rolling off the drawing board. Some were better than others. Part of the difficulty was that to prosper, they had to pander to the wishes of the rich purchaser, whether they agreed with them or not. Amateur interference with the professional designers had to be tolerated. The customer was always right. Despite this, some inkling of the success to follow came as, in 1924, the DH50, a highly successful civil version of the DH4, won the King's Cup Race around Britain. But it was the DH60, the Moth, that would set the seal on de Havilland's peacetime fame and give his company financial security.

Light, with a powerful engine, it had all the appearance of a winner, its sleek outline testimony to the saying, "if it looks well, it will fly well". De Havilland flew the prototype for the first time in February 1925. In May, Cobham flew it from Croydon to Zurich, some 500 miles, for lunch and home again in the afternoon, his flying time 13 hours 51 minutes, his average speed 70 mph. In 1926, a pair of Moths flew to Karachi while, in 1927, Flight Lieutenant Bentley made the first solo flight to Cape Town in a light aircraft, a Moth. Moths would win the King's Cup Races in 1926, 1927 and 1928. De Havilland Aircraft Company was on its way, nothing succeeding like success.

Flying clubs began to spring up around the country, some state aided, flying Moths in club colours. One of the earliest was the London Aeroplane Club at Stag Lane where many amateurs learned to fly. Cobham, with his "connections", began to fly wealthy patrons on pleasure trips to Europe. In 1925 he flew to Rangoon and back in a DH50. With him he took Sir Sefton Brancker, now Director of Civil Aviation, a brilliant organiser with a vision of

Britain's future in international flight, sadly to be killed in the R101 disaster of 1930. In 1925 and 1926 he would fly a DH50 to Cape Town and back, Melbourne and back, with no search after records but only to map out future commercial routes. An early result was the first scheduled international passenger service, flown from Hounslow to Le Bourget by these converted DH4 bombers. In 1926, the company survived two disappointments, one being Trenchard's decision to buy American Curtiss Fairey Foxes, the other the amicable departure of Alan Cobham, recently knighted, to run his own show. But such disappointments were to be more than discounted by the timely appearance of Alan Butler. A shrewd, rich man with an eye for adventure - he was also a transatlantic sailor - he also could recognise a good business risk when he saw one. He invested heavily in de Havilland's at the time of their greatest need to become a lifelong friend of the de Havilland family.

There was to be no shortage of competition in the search for glory in the skies. In May 1927, Charles Lindbergh, an American, won $25,000 when he flew solo non-stop from New York to Paris in 33 hours. As if not to be outdone, women, in the form of Lady Bailey, a mother of five children who had survived partial scalping when swinging a propeller, took a light plane to a record height of 17,283 feet. An intrepid lady, the first woman to fly solo to South Africa and back, bored of flying herself, later employed a chauffeur pilot to take her to foreign lands as she sat in the rear seat, knitting. The Duchess of Bedford, another of the London Aeroplane Club's favourite habitués, when informed that her licence was not to be renewed on account of her age, flew her Moth out over the east coast, never to be seen again. 1928 was also a year of records. Bert Hinkler, a crack Australian test pilot, made the first England to Australia solo flight in 15.5 days while another Australian, Charles Kingsford Smith, and his crew crossed the Pacific from Oakland,

California, to Brisbane in three "hops" via Honolulu and Fiji. Amelia Earhart, an American, made her first transatlantic crossing, as a passenger. It was high time de Havilland, an Englishman, got amongst the action. But how, now that Cobham had left?

Enter a young Yorkshire lass, a Sheffield University graduate and London secretary with a burning desire to fly. Amy Johnson spent her savings on flying lessons at Stag Lane. She took her pilot's licence and, for good measure, her ground engineer's licence, the first to be granted to a woman. Flying her beloved Gipsy Moth *Jason*, she took over where Cobham had left off, making herself and her plane household names. In May 1930, she became the first woman to fly solo from England to Darwin. The flight had already been completed eight times. Francis Chichester, also in a Gipsy Moth, had made the journey the previous January, having made a preliminary warm-up flight around Europe, again in a Gypsy Moth. Johnson's flight fell short of the record by some three days but perhaps her gallant failure only went to confirm her as the darling of the English speaking world, the "Queen of the Air" as the British press dubbed her. 200,000 people turned out to welcome her home to Croydon. In 1931, she flew across Siberia to Tokyo, in 1932, broke the solo record to Cape Town.

Everywhere she went, the name of de Havilland went with her. She and the plane "looked right" together, raising the sport of flying to a cult amongst the thoroughly modern woman. As a result, in 1930, Gipsy Moths won the Women's Pursuit Handicap, the Women's Air Derby, the Women's Dixie Derby, while Laura Ingalls challenged the men with a world record of 344 continuous loops. De Havilland built planes that were not only fast but strong.

Though its progeny, such as the Tiger Moth, would carry the name with honour for years to come, the Moth of the record breaking era ceased production in 1934, when de Havilland had other ideas to pursue. Speed was the current national obsession. Britons vied for the land speed record. British ships were in the van in the fight for the transatlantic Blue Riband. In the air, it was no different. Another gifted British designer, R.J. Mitchell, had won the Schneider Trophy in 1927 and in 1929. In 1931, he had won the Trophy outright, going on to win the world speed record at 407.5 mph, despite Trenchard's interference. Seemingly determined not to acknowledge the virtue of unsurpassed speed in military aircraft, Trenchard had, in 1927, opposed the decision to make the RAF responsible for manning the Trophy challenge even though it was being funded privately and would provide valuable experience for future fighter pilots. Under his influence, less than three weeks after the victory in 1929, flown by an RAF pilot, all Government support was withdrawn. Only the charitable intervention of Lady Houston, shaming the Government to change its mind over RAF manning, made outright victory in 1929 possible. But Mitchell's driving force was pure speed, the desire to go faster and faster. De Havilland, the bomber designer, would always have at the back of his mind, what would his plane also carry?

While Mitchell would go on, together with Sydney Camm of Hawkers and despite the deadweight of the Trenchard bomber philosophy, to produce the planes that would save Britain in 1940, where was de Havilland going to find the bomber to match? If fighters were going to fly that fast and speed was going to be the bomber's best defence, it must have been his dream to design a bomber that would fly even faster than 407.5 mph.

In 1925, the service chiefs were told by their political masters they need not expect a major war for the next 10 years, a "10 year rule" that was to be extended annually until 1928 when it was made

The Trenchard Touch

permanent, to be revoked only in 1932. This hardly created the urgent atmosphere needed to keep the services on their toes or to convince the taxpayer that vast sums of money should be lavished on them; after all, had not the last war been the war to end war? Against this, the general drift towards disarmament or, more accurately against rearmament, gained speed. Several Labour MPs saw armaments as being nothing more than requirements for "capitalist war". It was surprising then that it was Lord Haldane, a much underrated statesman but the real power behind Ramsey MacDonald's first Labour Government, who forced through the legislation to form the Auxiliary Air Force, comparable with the Territorial Army and one of Trenchard's dreams.

A new command for air defence was set up under the hero of Iraq, Sir John Salmond, though Trenchard made sure that Salmond's bomber squadrons outnumbered fighters by three to one. Salmond organised the first massed formation flights over London since the Gotha raids and military aircrews were encouraged to make long flights and take part in displays alongside the private competitors; anything to justify their existence and to keep the flyers at concert pitch. Younger commanders began to come through to challenge the top brass; Portal, Tedder, Slessor. Even so, it was difficult to justify what many saw as an expensive luxury and there must have been cause for relief when the Imam of Yemen kidnapped two sheiks claiming British protection and required to be "taught a lesson" while Harris could always be relied on to provide some action on the North West Frontier even if his planes had no tyres.

Churchill's defence cuts had resulted in the Bristol fighter remaining the standard Army co-operation aircraft, patched up DH9s, never de Havilland's most successful plane, the standard bomber. The RAF, though more secure than at any time in its short history, was languishing in the doldrums, watching with envy the advances in private flying. The annual Hendon Air Display gave them the opportunity to parade their skills in obsolescent aircraft but it left plenty of time for discussion and argument, perhaps too much time to Trenchard's way of thinking.

Home defence and Trenchard's philosophy needed constant reaffirmation for fear of some liberal lateral thinker undermining what was now accepted dogma. But how could any discussion take place without someone stating the counter argument? Could intelligent men be asked for years on end to solemnly repeat a creed without question? Limited discussions as to the possibility of defence in the air over home territory did occur amongst members of the Chiefs of Staff Committee, but always in private. With a "not in front of the servants" attitude, not even their respective Ministers were informed. In 1927, Trenchard had admitted, "... air fighting will be inevitable, but it will not take the form of a series of battles between the opposing air forces to gain supremacy as a first step ..." But to admit publicly even to having considered the possibility of air defence only weakened their adamantly stated position that the only feasible defence of the nation was terror bombing of the enemy.

As proclaimed by his early educational difficulties, Trenchard, as honest and brave as any man, was no intellectual, no academic. There is no way of knowing whether he ever read the works of Guilio Douhet, an Italian Army General and acknowledged father of strategic bombing. While Douhet was totally convinced that massive air attacks had the potential to decide the outcome of a war, he recognised the fact that the first stage, essential to success, was the preliminary destruction of the enemy's air defence. Trenchard's tunnel-visioned philosophy would not even contemplate the possibility of an effective air defence. Any bomber, sufficiently armed and armoured, would brush aside anything put up against it.

In 1928, Trenchard stated in a memo to his fellow Chiefs of Staff, a copy of which their Ministers were allowed to see, "For any army to defeat the enemy nation, it is almost always necessary as a preliminary step to defeat the enemy's army, which imposes itself as a barrier that must first be broken down. It is not, however, necessary for an air force, in order to defeat the enemy nation, to defeat its armed forces first. Air power can dispense with that immediate step, can pass over the enemy's navies and armies, and penetrate the air defences and attack direct the centres of production, transportation and communication from which the enemy's war effort is maintained. ... it will be in this manner that air superiority will be obtained and not by direct destruction of air forces."

While silent on the question of the morality of strategic bombing, Trenchard had no qualms as to its legitimacy. "Such objectives," he wrote, "may be situated in centres of population in which their destruction from the air will result in casualties also to the neighbouring civilian population ... The fact that air attacks may have that result is no reason for regarding the bombing as illegitimate ... Otherwise a belligerent would be able to secure immunity for his war manufacturers by locating them in a large city which would in effect become neutral territory."

This was the Gospel according to Marshal of the Royal Air Force, Hugh 'Boom' Trenchard, Baron of Wolfeton, when, on January 1, 1930, he retired. He had not won all his battles. His failure to convince the Imperial Defence Committee that aeroplanes would be far more effective in the defence of Singapore than 15-inch guns he would admit, in later life, to have been his biggest mistake. But he left his country's service an honoured and highly respected man. More significantly, he left behind him, not only an entrenched belief in the power of offensive bombing but a succession of disciples, brainwashed and faithful. Sir John Salmond, his natural successor, remained convinced that there was no effective way to defend one's country against air attack. Proof, if it was needed, that Salmond had kept up the good work was presented in 1932 by Stanley Baldwin. "The bomber," Baldwin said, "will always get through. The only defence is offence, which means you have to kill more women and children more quickly than the enemy if you want to save yourselves."

Trenchard must have been proud of his protégé who had prompted such a blood-curdling statement from the man who, as Lord President of the Council, was the true power behind MacDonald's coalition government. In 1933, Salmond was replaced by Edward Ellington, hardly the man to rock the boat. An intelligent man, his previous experience had been mainly in staff appointments in India, the Middle East and in Iraq. He had never flown operationally, had never commanded a squadron. Cautious, retiring and uninspiring, he was happy to accept the concept, forged on the anvil of war by those far more experienced than he, that the fighter could not defend against the bomber. In fact, when he took command of an air force reduced to 30,000 men, equipped with outdated machines, he had virtually no practical knowledge of aviation. The RAF was in this parlous state when, abroad, Germany walked out of the World Disarmament Conference, bringing about its final breakdown, while, at home, rearmament was proving a political vote loser. In a by-election in East Fulham, fought on an blatant disarmament ticket, a Labour candidate transformed a Tory majority of 14,000 into a Labour one of 5,000.

Prospects for the RAF could surely sink no lower.
Matters abroad were very different. Germany's military might was

beginning to strain at the shackles imposed on it by the Treaty of Versailles. The old Weimar hierarchy, élitist, effete, defeated, submissive, was being infiltrated with a new driving force of unforeseen evil. Restoration of national pride after the humiliation of Versailles was the understandable, to the more liberally-minded abroad even acceptable banner which only obscured far more threatening objectives of which parity with Britain on land and sea, reoccupation of the Rhineland and restoration of their colonies were but starting points in their search for *lebensraum*.

In January 1933, President Paul Ludwig Hans von Beneckendorff und Hindenberg, archetypal "old" Germany to his finger tips, was obliged to invite Herr Hitler, the ex-NCO and upstart Nazi leader, to become Chancellor and form a Cabinet. Within days a permanent state of emergency was declared and, by June, as disarmament swept candidates into the British Parliament, all German political parties were dissolved and the fond hopes of von Papen, the Vice Chancellor, that he could tame the firebrand Hitler, began to fade. The Army's reaction was ambivalent. General Kurt von Hammerstein-Equord, the Army commander in chief, together with the other politically inept supreme command, monocled, scar-faced Hindenberg clones, treated the jumped-up Austrian corporal with total disdain. Of one thing they were quite sure, Hitler was no gentleman.

Other officers saw the National Socialist movement as a tide of popularity which might sweep the Army back to its rightful place in German society. Some amongst the junior officers, such as Henning von Tresckow, Franz Halder and Hans Oster, had even in their youth campaigned on behalf of the Party. But whatever individual attitudes to the new Chancellor were, all, young and old, were united in their detestation of Hitler's sidekick, Ernst Röhm's SA. The Brownshirts, a murderous band of criminals, led by an arrogant, offensive psychopath, appeared to have been given by Hitler free rein in a para-military role that the regular Army viewed with alarm. Even so, a few Army officers had fancied their chances amongst the SA's ranks and changed from grey to brown.

For more than a year, Hitler retained power only because he was tolerated by the Army. In the presence of the Generals he was diffident, even obsequious, politically aware that united action on their parts would have been the end of him. Hindenberg was still commander in chief of all the German armed forces. One word from him and the Prussian-bred respect for an order would have galvanised the Army into sweeping Hitler from power, almost certainly to his death. Anxious on the one hand to appease and reassure the Generals, on the other to remove someone who was becoming a thorn from his flesh, Hitler acted. In June 1934, on the "night of the long knives", Röhm was murdered and his Brownshirts effectively destroyed. Two months later, Hindenberg died and, scarcely had he drawn his last breath, Hitler declared himself both Führer and Chancellor. As Führer he assumed immediately what he had always striven for, overall command of all German armed forces. On August 2, all officers swore an oath of allegiance, not to his office, but to Hitler personally. Hitler had won his first victory, over his own Army.

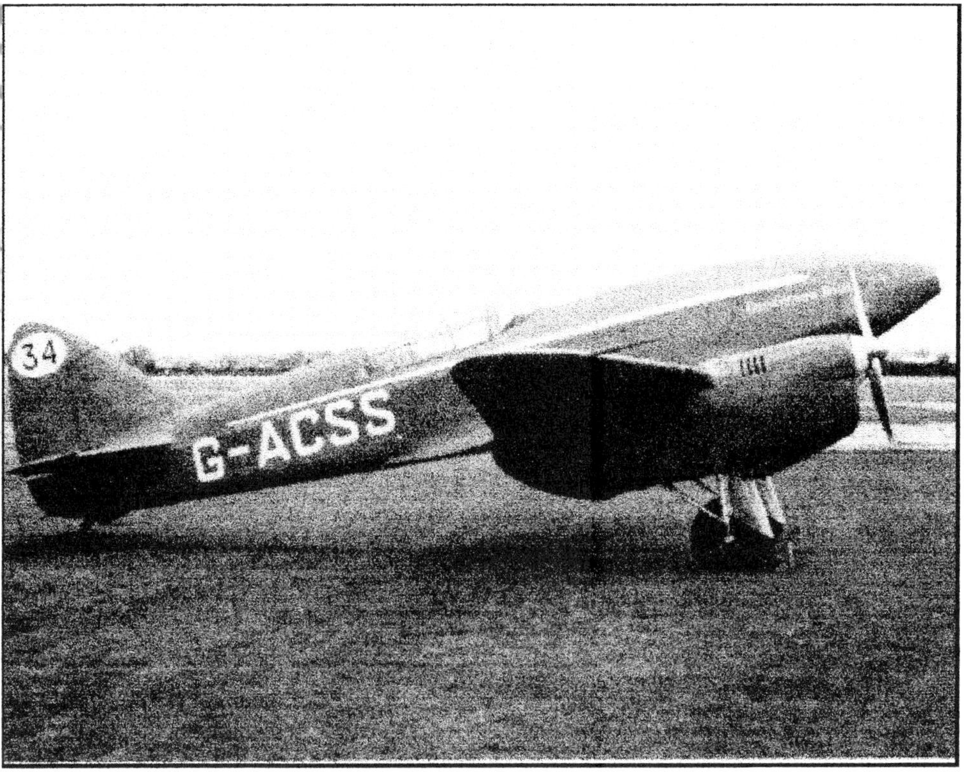
34
G-ACSS

Chapter Seven

Back in Britain, 1934 again saw aviation records tumble though at a slightly less frenetic pace. Jim Mollison flew 2,530 miles non-stop to Baghdad while Jean Batten, the snooty though undeniably beautiful New Zealander, took four days off Amy Johnson's time to fly solo from England to Australia. They made the headlines which obscured the more sinister events abroad. What was going on in Germany was a purely internal matter, no cause to deflect de Havilland from his next challenge. R.J. Mitchell may have had his days of glory. Now it was to be de Havilland's turn. Mitchell may have proved his ability to make aeroplanes fly very fast over short distances. But what about speed over thousands of miles?

Sir MacPherson Robertson, a wealthy Australian business man, had thrown down the gauntlet, offering to sponsor a race from Mildenhall in Suffolk to Melbourne Race Course; 11,333 miles. There were to be five mandatory stops on the way; Baghdad, Allahabad, Singapore, Port Darwin and Charleville. The MacRobertson Race, as it came to be known, would be open to any aircraft from any nation. Of the 70 planes entered, only 20 would take off, a mere nine stay the course. Of the motley group of craft entered, de Havilland feared but one, the American DC2, owned by the Royal Dutch Air Lines. A low winged cantilever monoplane of all metal construction, declared to be taking part in normal commercial trim with an everyday payload, it was given no chance. But de Havilland had that instinct about aircraft; to him the plane looked right and, if it looked right ... He was not sure he had a plane to match it. As a result, uniquely amongst the entrants, he decided to design and build a plane specifically for the race, a gigantic gamble in the time allowed.

In fact he would make three, offering them for sale at £5,000 apiece, well below the cost of construction, another huge gamble on the long-term benefit accruing to the company winning such a high profile race. He personally would design it, the DH88. It would have the sleekest line, the smoothest surface to minimise drag and it would be called the Comet. It would incorporate variable pitch propellers, retractable undercarriage and wing flaps, the first time all three features had been built into one aircraft. Its two engines would be Gipsy Sixes, modified by Frank Halford from the Gipsy Fours so successful on the DH Dragon Rapides. In-line, as compared with the DC2's radials, these would be set into the wings as aerodynamically as possible, again to reduce drag to a minimum. Like the DC2, it also would be a low wing cantilever monoplane but with one portentous difference; the whole airframe would be of wooden construction. Arthur Hagg had a hobby which, in later life, would become his livelihood; he built boats. Applying the principles of boat building to aircraft, the Comet's wings would be made from strips of spruce, arranged in two layers which ran at right angles to each other. Such was the rush to complete on time, Hubert Broad, the test pilot, was allowed flights of 10 to 15 minutes only between adjustments. But no major snags were found. It flew like a comet.

Now all de Havilland had to do was to sell them.

It seemed only natural that Amy Johnson and Jim Mollison should buy one they called "Black Magic". They were to fail, putting down in Karachi with engine trouble. A rich man, Bernard Rubin, bought another and employed pilots Cathcart-Jones and Waller to fly it. They were third across the line. The last was bought by A.O. Edwards to publicise his Grosvenor House Hotel. His pilots, Charles Scott and Tom Campbell Black, relatively unknown before the race, became household names overnight as they won in just under 71 hours flying time at an average speed of 159 mph.

The triumph boosted a whole nation's morale. With Mitchell's

Supermarine S6B and now the Comet, Britain possessed the two fastest planes on earth. Admittedly the fact that the DC2 with a normal payload had come a close second and had won the race on handicap, was played down in Britain. That was only natural but the experts were not fooled. They saw in the DC2's all metal cantilever monoplane with its cowled engines the commercial airliner of the future; witness its beloved successor, the DC3 Dakota. But, surely, there must have been others, equally expert, who should have seen the military potential of the Comet. There were already those who saw Mitchell's planes as the fighters of the future. Could no one see in the Comet the bomber of the future?

The Comet was still flying in 1938 when, with a range now of 2,800 miles and a speed of 225 mph at 19,000 feet, it flew to New Zealand and back, a distance of 26,000 miles in 11 days. The other two Comets had already been bought by the French and Portuguese Air Forces, only too anxious to learn from de Havilland's expertise. But the British Air Ministry, blinded by Trenchard's vision of what a bomber should look like if it was going to "slug it out" all the way to the target, disregarded it completely. Perhaps they could not bring themselves to visualise such a beautiful aircraft being used "... to kill more women and children more quickly than the enemy ..."Whatever their thinking might have been, they allowed this sleek triumph of British engineering to end up a pile of junk hidden from view beneath a tarpaulin on the edge of Gravesend airfield.

By March 1935, Reichsmarschal Goering felt sufficiently confident to announce to the world that Germany now possessed an air force, the Luftwaffe, in international political theory still an illegal act. Hitler went further, boasting to Sir John Simon, the British Foreign Secretary, that they already had parity in the air with Britain. It was not true. Though they were producing some 100 military aircraft a month with a stockpile of 400, they were still far short of parity in numbers but their designs were well in advance of the obsolete British. But it was enough to concentrate a few minds in Whitehall the only result of which was a plan to negotiate with Germany with a view to outlawing aerial bombing; with predictable results.

In June 1935, Stanley Baldwin returned as Prime Minister but little changed. If a niggling fear of German resurgent power existed, there was little or no political manifestation of it. That maverick, Winston Churchill, still languished in the political wilderness, occupying a restless mind in writing as, in his epic work on Marlborough, he strove to restore respectability to his ancestors. Considered too clever by far, up there amongst the likes of Lloyd-George and F.E. Smith, he once again failed to gain office when Baldwin formed his Cabinet. Baldwin might have been wiser had he given Churchill some minor ministerial post where he could control him. As it was, Churchill felt free to criticise Baldwin at every turn. He chose to spearhead his attack with German rearmament, particularly in the air. The facts and theories with which Churchill plagued Baldwin were provided by a faithful ally, an irascible Oxford physics professor, Frederick Lindemann. Their military intelligence, gleaned from Germany, frequently outclassed that of the Government both in quantity and in accuracy and Churchill's well-informed nagging was becoming intolerable to a Prime Minister who had other things on his mind. He was otherwise busily employed co-operating with the French Premier, Pierre Laval, in giving Fascist Italy a free hand in Ethiopia while, at home, the name of Wallis Warfield Simpson was being linked with the young king. Alongside such weighty matters, what did it signify that, in March, Hitler had realised the first of his dreams when, with a handful of poorly trained German units, he had reoccupied the demilitarised Rhineland, except that it only went to sharpen Churchill's attacks.

Ultimately, Baldwin could bear Churchill's goadings no longer. Along the lines of making a gamekeeper out of your most persistent poacher, Baldwin appointed Churchill to a secret committee on air defence research. Lindemann's expertise would now be given the power of astute political influence.

Meanwhile, Jean Batten had flown solo from England to Argentina, Amelia Earhart solo from Hawaii to California. But it all seemed less important than in years past. There were other things to think about, such as how dangerously low Britain had let its guard fall. No longer was rearmament altogether a dirty word.

The mood swing towards rearmament in 1936 was not universal. The Cabinet stoutly resisted the Secretary of State for War, Duff Cooper's demand to modernise 12 Territorial Divisions. It was still widely believed that Germany could not possibly be ready for war before 1942 and Neville Chamberlain, the Chancellor of the Exchequer, held that Germany was far more likely to be defeated in the economic world than on the field of battle. In his opinion, "The political temper of the people of this country is strongly opposed to Continental adventures." For all that, Scheme F for the expansion of the RAF - there had been a series of ineffective schemes dating back to Scheme A in 1934 - was forced through Cabinet. The proportions of bomber squadrons to fighter, based on the still almost universally accepted precept that there was no such thing as an effective air defence, was to be 5:2.

Edward Ellington was still Chief of the Air Staff. While no one doubted his intelligence or questioned his courage, due to his lack of "hands on" experience his ability to recognise a good aircraft when he saw one was a matter for concern. It was fortunate for him and, for that matter, for the country as a whole, that over him at a crucial time he had a most competent Secretary of State for Air, Lord Swinton, while below him served many middle-aged career officers with operational experience and destined for high office. They included Cyril Newall, commander of the specialised bomber squadron in WW1, Hugh Dowding, the fighter expert, Arthur Harris, home from the Northwest Frontier, and Arthur Tedder. And one other, Wilfrid Freeman, the man who had narrowly escaped death in the first few days of WW1 and had gone on to command a DH4 bomber squadron.

The standard bombers of the day were the Hawker Harts and Hinds, pretty little biplanes but hardly likely to strike terror into the hearts of the German man in the street. It was accepted that these must be replaced by the Bristol Blenheim, the Handley Page Hampden and the Fairey Battle, planes scarcely more terrifying to look at, particularly the Battle. As to the "heavies", planning was already in hand for the Wellington, a Barnes Wallis's brainchild, and the Whitley. These would be allowed to proceed. There were signs now of underlying panic. The order was given for large-scale production of the Whitley long before the prototype flew, the first production model rolling off the assembly line almost simultaneously with the prototype staggering into the air. The Wellington, in its way, would serve the RAF well but the Whitley, of which nearly 1,500 were built and needing a crew of five, proved slow with a limited range, bomb load and ceiling.

That was the bomber force as visualised when, in July 1936, the Air Staff were finally permitted to state their requirements for the bombers that would be needed if they were to prosecute Trenchard's "active defence" of Britain in the war that was becoming increasingly inevitable. As a result, Air Ministry

Specification B. 12/36 laid down the criteria for the heavy bomber, P. 13/36 the medium. Two development contracts were allotted for the heavy bomber, one to Short and Harland, the other to R.J. Mitchell at Supermarine. Mitchell's prototype would be destroyed in an early air raid on Southampton and it will never be known whether he was as good at designing bombers as he undoubtedly was at fighters. The plane that emerged from Shorts, the Stirling, the first of the four engined heavies, was doomed to mediocrity before it left the drawing board. The standard hanger doors of the day were 100 feet wide. The Stirling's wingspan, reduced in width to conform, gave good manoeuvrability but grossly limited its ceiling. If required to fly to Italy, it would have to fly through the Alps rather than above them. The mid-mounted wings demanded an over long undercarriage, making take off with a full load very hazardous. To cap it all, though capable of lifting 14,000 lbs, due to an insoluble design fault the biggest individual bomb it could carry was 1,000 lbs. Its maiden flight in May 1939 ended in disaster as its undercarriage collapsed on landing but, like the Whitley, production had already commenced before anyone knew how it flew. In operation, the Stirling, with a climbing speed of roughly 150 mph, would prove an ineffective, lumbering death trap for its crew of seven.

Specification P. 13/36 required a two engined, self-protecting medium bomber with a range of 3,000 miles, a 4,000 lb bomb load and a speed of 275 mph at 15,000 feet. Ambitious figures at that time. A bewildered Ellington saw two contracts awarded on these criteria. The accepted Handley Page design HP56 never materialised but HP57 would go on to become the Halifax. With a cruising speed of just over 200 mph, it would take two years for the prototype to fly, three years before the first production model took to the air in October 1940. In operational use nearly half as many planes would be lost on test or training flights as by enemy action. The other contract went to A.V. Roe for their Type 679, to be known as the Manchester. It would be May 1940 before the second prototype flew, the first having crashed at Boscombe Down almost a year previously. Some 12 squadrons would ultimately be equipped with 200 Manchesters but they played no effective part in air strategy and have been largely forgotten.

But, just as de Havilland was the design genius behind his firm and Vickers had their Barnes Wallis, so at Avro was a man called Chadwick. It was obvious that, long before the Manchester even reached the prototype stage, Chadwick had lost all real faith in it, for, in the autumn of 1938, his thoughts turned away from the Manchester to a much more powerful four engined design. Chadwick was the embodiment of the Trenchard dream, a man who could deliver an instrument of mass destruction. Whitley, Stirling, Halifax, Manchester; the names of northern towns were much in favour. Why not then call Chadwick's creation the Lancaster?

It is difficult to analyse what goes towards making a good designer, virtually impossible when considering a creative genius. That a certain minimal knowledge of mathematics, physics and aerodynamics are required is obvious but behind every designer is a team of draughtsmen, aerodynamicists, stress experts and engineers to bring down flights of fancy into the realms of reality. But in design, what separates the gifted from the merely competent defies description. In many ways their creations are manifestations of their inner beings, their machines, constructed from wood and metal, no less the result of artistic flair than the sculptor's figure hewn from a chunk of stone. De Havilland already had a string of past designs that clung to principles of grace and beauty. To have asked de Havilland to design a fearsome, awe inspiring monster would have been like asking Mozart to write an atonal symphony.

But though now financially stable - the swing towards rearmament had resulted in a steady stream of orders for the Tiger Moth trainer alone - the demand for civil aircraft was slowing. The disappearance of Amelia Earhart into the Pacific Ocean raised hardly a ripple in the newspapers this side of the Atlantic. It was time to think of military aircraft again. A second generation DH4 perhaps?

On September 1, 1937, Cyril Newall was appointed Chief of Air Staff. Ellington, an able man but out of his depth, was replaced by the most experienced operational bomber commander of WW1. He did not take long to make his presence felt. The RAF was by now divided into Fighter, Bomber and Coastal Commands. To the post of C in C Bomber Command, Newall appointed Edgar Ludlow-Hewitt, another distinguished wartime squadron commander who had proved his peacetime diplomatic skills also when acting as facilitator between Trenchard and his Secretary of State, Samuel Hoare. Between them, they submitted to Cabinet Scheme J which refined the Trenchard concept to the point of a "knock out blow". Sir Thomas Inskip, the Minister for Co-ordination of Defence, considered the RAF incapable of such an attack, claiming that Britain's only hope in the event of aerial attack was to prevent the Germans from delivering their own "knock out blow". Inskip, with cold reason on his side, won the day in Cabinet, resulting in Scheme K with more emphasis on fighter aircraft. Anyway, Inskip argued, fighters were cheaper to make than bombers. Trenchard was not slow to make Newall acquainted with his views on the matter. Retirement had done nothing to neuter Trenchard. Hore-Belisha, the new Secretary of State for War, a Jew with no reason to love the Germans, had been persuaded by Weir, still an *éminence grise*, to take on Trenchard as his War Office adviser. The fact that Trenchard was stripped of all executive clout did not prevent him from making his views public in characteristic fashion. Obliged to be a reluctant supporter of the current atmosphere of appeasement, knowing the country was in no position to take any other stance, his basic philosophy remained unchanged. "The only thing," he stated, "that will stop warmongers is the knowledge that, if they attack, they will be hit harder than they themselves can hit." Newall must have also feared for Trenchard's reaction when he found out that the Admiralty, his fiercest competitor in years past, had finally been given command of the Fleet Air Arm.

For all the command changes and thickening war clouds, rearmament proceeded at a snail's pace. A nation, commercially prosperous, was reluctant to divert its energies into preparation for a war it fondly hoped might never come. What rearmament occurred was patchy. Remembering the engine shortage of 1914, it was easier to obtain an engine than an airframe as Austin, Rootes, Rover, Standard, Daimler, all were prepared for war. It was against this background of grinding inertia that de Havilland, accompanied by Charles Walker, knocked on the Air Ministry door, finally to be admitted into the presence of a pair of bureaucratic buffoons.

The one Comet Racer remaining in Britain was still flying, its power and speed very much in the de Havilland design team's mind. The DH4 bomber had owed much of its success to the fact that no enemy fighter could catch it. Contemporary fighter speeds were steadily creeping above the 300 mph mark. The solution seemed obvious. The 400 mph bomber must be constructed, something along the lines of the Comet but much more powerful. The power to weight ratio would be crucial. One sixth of the loaded weight of the conventional bomber of the day was accounted for by its defensive armament. De Havilland's bomber, made of wood of course, would have no defensive armament. Its speed and its ceiling would be its defence. As crucial as the power to weight ratio would be the problem of drag. With no turrets or machine guns to mar its aerodynamic streamlining, it would need no more than a crew of two, a pilot and a bomb aimer/navigator, rather than the "normal" seven. With the most basic of drawings outlining their vision of the bomber of the future, de Havilland and Walker put their case.

But it proved too simple, logical and imaginative for the tortuous rigidity of the ministerial mind, already brainwashed with years of Trenchard's teachings. The planners were wedded to the four engined heavy bomber as the only possible means of transforming strategic theory into awful reality. Had not the Americans already led the way? Across the Atlantic, squadrons were being equipped with the B17, an impregnable flying fortress of a plane with a crew of 10, maybe 11. How possibly could a twin engined plane, made of wood and with a crew of two, compete? The drawings were scarcely glanced at, a man of de Havilland's pedigree invited patronisingly to co-operate instead with the development of the wing for some nebulous experimental plane called "The Ape".Such a rebuff would have disheartened a lesser man. But de Havilland was the true originator, someone who would rather create than eat. Denied all official backing, he returned to his friends, determined to make the DH98 and to hell with the Ministry.

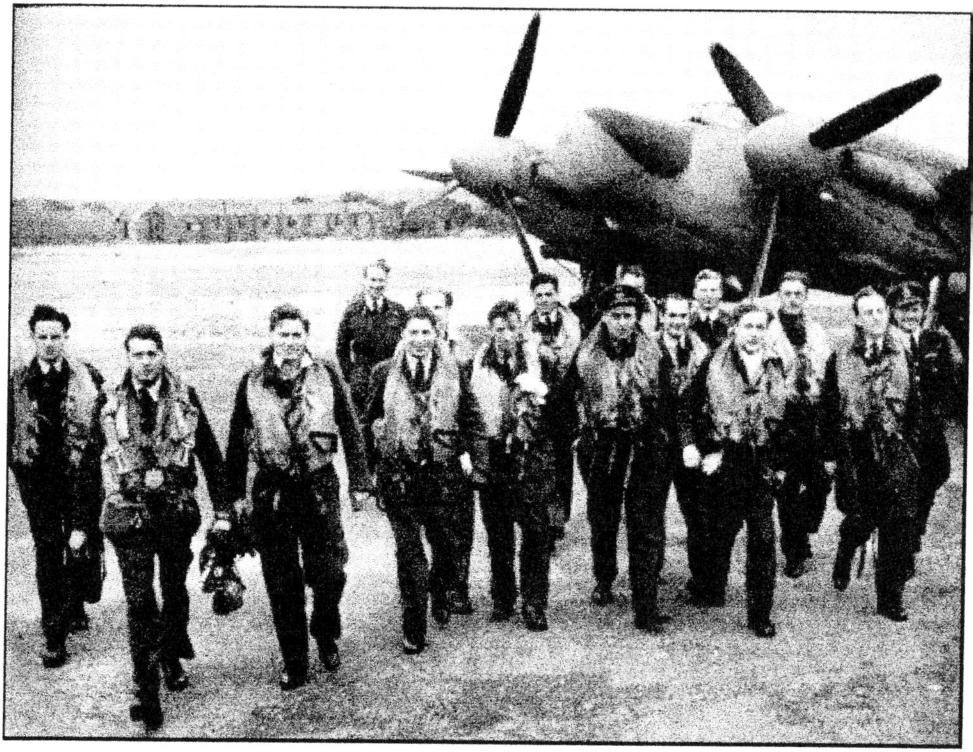

Chapter Eight

Resistance to Hitler by the Army had, for the most part, taken the form of passive disdain. If they ignored the low-bred upstart long enough, perhaps he would go away. It was true that Hitler's elimination of Röhm and his Brownshirts had sharpened the Generals' perception of just how vicious and ruthless their new lord and master was. But, before the apolitical, professional soldiers could take stock, they had found themselves ordered by "old rubber lion" General Werner von Blomberg, the Wehrmacht Commander in Chief and Minister for War, to swear an oath of allegiance, not to an office of President, whoever that might be, but to Hitler himself, the Führer. For a professional soldier of any army to swear allegiance, be it to Crown or President, is a matter of some consequence. To the Prussian, noted for his blind obedience, it was a matter of honour, any act, almost any word, revealing second thoughts a matter of dishonour. If there was a conflict between conscience and duty, duty must prevail. Having sworn the oath, any act, designed to bring down Hitler, would, in the minds of the vast majority of the officer corps be nothing short of treason, punishable by death.

That did not preclude criticism, on a purely apolitical, professional basis of course, of Hitler's military strategy. There was widespread belief amongst the Generals that Hitler was determined to go to war. They were not essentially opposed to the idea. They relished the chance of restoring the glory of the German Army after its humiliation at Versailles. Their anxiety was that he should provoke a war with another major power, particularly Britain, before they were fully prepared. Most anxious about Hitler's military intentions was General Ludwig Beck, the Army Chief of Staff. But Beck, the "philosopher general", while of undoubted integrity but equally as inept politically as his brother Generals, was sorely troubled with a soldier's loyalty. Submissively, he stood back as Hitler ordered his troops into the Rhineland, the nation's euphoria at the successful venture, giving Hitler the chance to deal with his Generals once and for all.

Baron Werner von Fritsch was Commander in Chief of the Army. On a charge of homosexuality, backed up by the Gestapo with paid false witnesses, von Fritsch was disgraced without one of his brother officers raising a finger in his defence. Though cleared later by a military court of honour, Fritsch never recovered and would die honourably on the field of battle. But his engineered dismissal was Hitler's opportunity to assume direct command of the Army and purge his High Command of the old guard. For good measure, he sacked his Foreign Secretary, von Neurath, who had opposed entry into the Rhineland, replacing him with the hard liner, von Ribbentrop.

The Wehrmacht's High Command, now stiffened with pro-Nazi Generals, stripped of what little political influence it had, stood by in awe as Hitler proceeded to annexe Austria with hardly a shot being fired. But his plans, widely circulated amongst the Generals, to militarily invade Czechoslovakia, was another matter altogether.

There were some in Germany, a courageous few, able to overcome their qualms over a soldier's loyalty. One such person was Hans Oster, the son of a Dresden parson, taught from childhood what was right and what was wrong. As a counter-intelligence expert, he had joined the Ministry of Defence in 1935 with the nominal rank of Lieutenant Colonel. By 1938, he had risen to become the Chief of the Central Division of the Military Intelligence Bureau, the Abwehr, when Hitler replaced Fritsch with Wilhelm Keitel, creating the High Command of the Oberkommando der Wehrmacht. Described as "decisive, quick witted and diplomatically imaginative", he saw quite clearly that his final duty was to his country. Equally clearly he saw in Hitler a psychopathic megalomanic who would ultimately bring Germany to its knees. Hitler must be stopped, a conviction only reinforced by the public humiliation of his old regimental commander, Werner von Fritsch. Devious to the point of recklessness, he used the resources of the Intelligence Services, between 1935 and 1938, to seek out and recruit like-minded patriots, one of them proving to be his own overall boss at OKW, Admiral Wilhelm Canaris.

An obvious possible recruit was Beck, the one general Hitler feared as carrying sufficient respect in the country to assume the Presidency should Hitler be toppled. Beck had sent Hitler numerous memoranda begging him to give up all idea of invading Czechoslovakia, warning him that Germany was in no position to wage war with Britain, should they intervene. Oster put it to Beck that the most effective, bloodless method of removing Hitler would be by mass resignation of all the Generals. But Beck argued that there were already too many pro-Nazis amongst them to risk failure and lose all anti-Nazi influence in the High Command. Beck's only solution was to resign himself, to take a step back while urging others to act. Hitler replaced Beck with Franz Halder. Unabashed, Oster went to work on Halder, getting at least an agreement from him that he would not stand in the way of any coup.

The patchy nature of the resistance was difficult to overcome. Groups sprang up here and there, usually the creation of individuals, often in ignorance of each other. They were separated not only by long distances with difficult, often perilous communications, but by their differences in motivation, be it religious, political, military or simply humanist. Political intrigue engendered strange bedfellows as communists strove to find common ground with the church or extreme right wing in their singleness of purpose. Unification into one large effective force was impossible, making the task of the Gestapo easier as it mopped up the isolated groups. As early as 1935, the socialist resistance group, Beginning Anew, was eliminated. Liquidation of the Red Fighters and the Socialist Front in Hanover, the largest of the resistance groups under Werner Blumenberg, followed. Outspoken men of God were arrested by the hundred.

Undaunted, Oster set about strengthening his group. A significant step forward was the recruitment of Erwin von Witzleben, the commander of the Berlin Military District. His support would be critical in dealing with the SS. Halder now asked Oster for details of his plans, still anxious that the removal of "the very incarnation of evil" should not have the appearance of mutiny; Hitler must be brought to justice, not killed by mob rule. Halder approved Oster's plans, pledging himself to support the coup but only if Hitler carried out his threat to invade Czechoslovakia. Of one thing, all - Halder, Oster, Witzleben, Canaris - were agreed; any coup was doomed to failure if it did not have the wholehearted support of the British. Only the fear of an all out war with Britain would be sufficient to win over enough of the Generals to ensure success. Efforts must be made to obtain confirmation of that support.

Ewald von Kleist-Schmenzin, the man chosen by Oster to approach the British, was a wealthy, Christian, conservative lawyer, a monarchist at heart, as near British as a German could come. Courageous and worldly, he had pleaded with Hindenberg in vain not to appoint Hitler as Chancellor. In London he spoke to Lloyd-George and Churchill, one with power in the past, one with power to come, neither with the power to help at that time, though Churchill gave Kleist a letter for his co-conspirators, saying he could not believe that Britain and France would not march. "Do not, I pray you," he wrote in typical Churchillian style, "be misled upon this point." But hopes ran high for the interview at the

Foreign Office with Sir Robert Gilbert Vansittart, the expert on Germany and a noted Germanophobe. But it seemed that Vansittart's hatred of the Germans extended to all Germans, pro- or anti-Nazi, even if Kleist had come pleading "with a rope around my neck." Beck had told Kleist, "Bring me back certain proof that England will fight if Czechoslovakia is attacked and I will put an end to this regime." But Kleist returned empty-handed.

An industrialist, Hans Bohm-Tettelbach followed in Kleist's footsteps with similar results. Oster's next emissary, Theo Kordt, on the staff of the German Embassy in London, actually gained access to 10, Downing Street, albeit via the back door, to have a long conversation with Lord Halifax, the Foreign Secretary, and to leave with high but equally false hopes.

Carl Goerdeler, Mayor of Leipzig, steeped in conservatism, fighting in virtual isolation, decided to oppose the regime from within. He had refused to raise the swastika over the Town Hall but had been obliged to stand and watch as the statue to Felix Mendelssohn, a genius but a wealthy Jew, was removed from in front of the Gewandhaus concert hall. In his position of Reich Commissioner for Price Control, he was able to travel abroad, canvassing for support. He too saw Vansittart who simply accused him of treason. "The same sort of ambitions are sponsored by a different body of men, and that is about all," Vansittart wrote. However, as if to demonstrate that there was nothing xenophobic in their attitude to the Germans' offers to eliminate Hitler, they were equally dismissive of an offer made by Colonel Noel Mason-MacFarlane, MC and two bars, Military Attaché at the British Embassy in Berlin, who had plans to shoot Hitler during a forthcoming parade, firing from his apartment's bathroom window. The Foreign Office refused him permission to proceed on the grounds that such a method would be "unsportsmanlike".

The underlying truth of the matter was that Chamberlain and his Cabinet had already resolved on handing Czechoslovakia to Hitler in pursuit of their policy of appeasement. Sir Nevile Henderson, the debonair British Ambassador, had already been instructed by Chamberlain to establish a secret personal contact with the Führer while Chamberlain dismissed Kleist and the others from his mind, describing them as modern day Jacobites, hoping to restore the past with British help.

It says a great deal for their courage that, despite the series of humiliating rebuffs from London, Oster's group decided to "go it alone" in the fond hope, even belief that Britain could not possibly stand aside and watch Czechoslovakia be invaded. Everything was now arranged. Beck had promised to become President. Halder, assured by Oster at OKW of at least 24 hours notice of Hitler's decision to invade Czechoslovakia, would be in overall military command. Erich Kordt, brother of Theo and leader of a resistance group within the German Foreign Office, would arrange for the great doors of the Chancellery to be opened while inside, some of the Generals including Karl-Heinrich von Stulpnagel, even Walther von Brauchitsch, nervous at Hitler's brinkmanship, had agreed to co-operate. Von Witzleben, now pledged the support of the commanders of the Potsdam garrison and an armoured division, was more than prepared to deal with the Führer's SS bodyguard while the task force itself would be led by Captain Friedrich Wilhelm Heinz, a soldier itching for a fight in any cause. And Hitler was to be shot while resisting arrest, that was now agreed by all. All that was required now was for the British to stand firm.

The news that Chamberlain, meeting Hitler at Berchtesgaden, was wavering caused alarm amongst the group. A second visit by the British Prime Minister did nothing to reassure. Neither did a statement from General Ironside, the British CIGS, that "It would be madness to expose ourselves to annihilation for the sake of the Czechs." Towards the end of September, as in London trenches were being dug, school children evacuated and hospitals cleared for action in readiness for the German "knock out blow" so feared by the Air Staff, so there was great anxiety amongst the German Generals that, this time, Hitler had gone too far and a great war, for which they were not prepared, was about to begin. Such was the secrecy with which the British Cabinet had cloaked their true intentions. The final surrender by Chamberlain at Munich on September 30 brought delight to Hitler, incredulous relief to the Generals and total devastation to the conspirators. To Oster, Halder and the others, it was obvious now there would be no war with Britain, only a surge of German national pride under Hitler's leadership and the hopes of a very brave band of men disappeared in the ashes of their plans, burnt in von Witzleben's fireplace.

The September plot was over.

London's urban sprawl had engulfed Stag Lane. What had served de Havilland well in the twenties was being slowly smothered. An aerial reconnaissance north of London, carried out in a Moth, had revealed what appeared suitable from the air; level farmland near Hatfield. Stag Lane had been sold, the farm bought, an architect employed and the transition made. The London Aeroplane Club had been the first to move, the production side waiting for custom-built workshops to be completed. Alan Butler, de Havilland's early benefactor, had taken over the farm and soon planes had been taking off and landing from an airfield surrounded by pedigree herds. In July 1934, de Havilland had taken off from Stag Lane for the last time.

In 1938, de Havillands was a well established, highly respected firm of aircraft manufacturers. Even so, as de Havilland and Walker returned from London, to build a revolutionary warplane without a vestige of official support was no mean undertaking. At least there would be no problems with the quality of the team de Havilland had around him. Alongside Walker, the engineer, Ronald Bishop, a man who had learned his craft from Arthur Hagg, would be Chief Designer. Richard Clarkson would look after the aerodynamics, Robert Harper the stress problems. The basic design concept, facilitated by total agreement throughout the team, was simple enough. Twin engined - Rolls Royce Merlins, of course - it would be a low wing monoplane, of wooden construction with a crew of two, sitting side by side, and with no defence armament. Speed was to be its only defence and all design was to be to that end. The four hundred mph aeroplane, capable of bombing Berlin in daylight; that was to be the target.

Over the ensuing months, the earliest drawings began to take shape when, in August 1938, just as the British Government was turning a deaf ear to Oster's pleas for help, de Havilland saw his first ray of hope. Wilfrid Freeman, now Air Marshal Sir Wilfrid Freeman, was made Air Member for Development and Production. Great mutual respect had existed between the two men, dating back to 1916 when de Havilland had frequently stayed at Freeman's DH4 squadron HQ in France. But Freeman had been more than an experienced bomber pilot and commander, being no fool when it had come to technical problems also. It had been largely due to him that the RAF, after the war, had developed the use of the variable pitch propeller and 100 octane fuel. But, as de Havilland would have been only too well aware, Freeman had also been in the fore in the campaign for the four engined heavy bombers and was favourably disposed towards Roy Chadwick at Avro with his plans for the Lancaster. It had been perhaps Freeman's one mistake that, in the frantic rush to rearm, he had urged the production of the earlier heavy bombers off the drawing board before they had been fully evaluated.

But it took just one short meeting with Freeman to convince him of the merits of the DH98. It was a measure of Freeman's ability to think laterally that, despite his faith in the four engined heavies, he could see the potential of what de Havilland had in mind. Many times he must have been grateful for the DH4's speed and had the vision to see an alternative to the "slug it out" leviathan. Without waiting for any authority from the Air Council and in the full knowledge that the Luftwaffe had already abandoned their experiments with laminated wooden construction, he pledged his full support for a plane which would become known at the Air Ministry as "Freeman's Folly". It was said to be too late to design and build a completely new aeroplane for "this" war that was coming. De Havilland was determined to prove them wrong.

All this against a background strategic philosophy unchanged despite Newall's Scheme K which had temporarily shifted the emphasis from bombing attack to fighter defence. Trenchard, now a frank embarrassment to Newall, had written to the Cabinet, stating that while fighters might possibly provide some degree of aerial defence, they would never win the war. Newall was obliged as a result to produce Scheme L with its return to priority for bomber production, arguing half-heartedly in the scheme's defence that "... no one can say with absolute certainty that a nation can be knocked out from the air only because no one has yet attempted it." The Air Staff memorandum that followed the Cabinet adoption of Scheme L must have made Trenchard breathe a sigh of relief. Targets, the memorandum stated, were to be divided into "precise targets" and "target groups", the earliest official euphemism for area bombing. The true target was to be the morale of the industrial worker rather than the factory where he worked. No mention was made of any prior necessity such as the destruction of the enemy air force.

Any creative driving force, such as a design team, needs peace and tranquillity to prosper. Some of de Havilland's planes had been designed in such places as attics in Fisherman's Walk, near Bournemouth, far removed from the bustle of Stag Lane. Salisbury Hall, an old moated country mansion, just five miles from Hatfield, said to harbour the ghost of Nell Gwynne, would be ideal for the design of DH98, now to be known as the Mosquito. Sheds and a hangar were built alongside in which the prototype would be constructed.

Drawing boards were set up in the main hall, Bishop's first drawing being no more than a free hand, thick pencil outline of a mental picture. Subsequent drawings would become finer and finer but often great skill was required turning rough outlines into component parts. Soon a mock up took shape and was hung from the ceiling of the vast kitchen. At least now they had something three dimensional to look at.

When war came in September 1939, Britain braced itself for the aerial onslaught everyone had been warned to expect. Back in 1936, official Air Staff estimates of German bombing capabilities had been 600 tons per day with 150,000 casualties in the first week. In 1939, that estimate had been upgraded to 700 tons with an initial "knock out blow" of 3,500 tons in the first 24 hours. The truth was very different. The Luftwaffe was fully occupied in Poland, carrying out what the Germans still considered its primary role, unchanged since the 1914-18 war, that of Army co-operation. The British Government, conned by Hitler and Goering, had also overestimated the German bomber strength. Even so, the 2,130 German front line bombers outnumbered British Bomber Command by 4:1.

The Manchester was proving totally inadequate, resulting in a draft proposal for Type 680, a four engined version, to be abandoned before it started. The maiden flight of the Stirling had ended in disaster. The Halifax had not yet flown. The Lancaster, required to have eight 20mm cannon and two enormous turrets, was still little more than a specification, B.1/39. And so the RAF took to the skies against the enemy with the single engined Battle and the twin engined Blenheims, Whitleys, Hampdens and Wellingtons. Less than half these planes were capable of reaching the Ruhr, fully loaded; not one could dream of bombing Berlin. Neville Chamberlain could well pronounce in the House of Commons that "Whatever be the lengths to which others may go, His Majesty's Government will never resort to the deliberate attack on women and children and other civilians for purposes of mere terrorism." Easy to say when your air force is totally incapable of carrying out any such campaign.

Edgar Ludlow-Hewitt, Bomber Command's Commander in Chief, was in no doubt as to the capabilities of the aircraft under his command. An outstanding fighter pilot of WW1, a man of high intellect and integrity, he had been foolish and brave enough in July to issue a stark warning. "As things are at present," he had stated, "the gunners have no real confidence in their ability to use their equipment efficiently in war and captains and crew have, I fear, little confidence in the ability of the gunners to defend them against destruction by enemy aircraft. Under these conditions it is unreasonable to expect these crews to press forward to their objectives in the face of heavy attack by fighters." He had gone on to inform his political masters that, if the bombers were ordered to make an all out daylight offensive, without fighter escort, the

Blenheims would be destroyed in three-and-a-half weeks, the heavies totally destroyed in seven-and-a-half weeks.

But Newall and the Air Council chose not to listen. A lone voice, even that of the Commander in Chief, crying in the wilderness, had little chance of being heard while echoes of Trenchard's Boom still thundered around. They would have to learn the hard way at the expense of the lives of many brave young men.

Daylight raids began immediately. On September 3, the first day of the war, 18 Hampdens set out to bomb the German Fleet in the Schillig Roads but failed to reach the target, jettisoning their bombs in the North Sea as they returned home. Within days of the declaration of war, seven out of 29 Blenheims and Wellingtons were shot down on coastal raids where instructions had been given to bring bombs home rather than risk German civilian casualties, this for no higher moral principle than the fear of reprisal raids. Before the end of the month, five out of 11 Hampdens did not return; in December, five out of 12 Wellingtons; then six out of 12; then 10 out of 24. With a bomb load of 4,000 lbs, the Wellington could not climb above 12,000 feet. With a speed of 165 mph, it would spend over two minutes within range of an individual 88 mm flack gun, longer if there was a head wind. The crunch came on December 18th when 22 Wellingtons, caught in formation in clear skies, lost 15 of their number.

Before the end of 1939 all unescorted daylight bombing raids were abandoned. Within a few months of war's outbreak, all faith in the heavily armoured, daylight, unescorted mass formation was in tatters. The heavily armoured bomber, it was patently obvious, struggling against the drag induced by turrets and guns, could not "slug it out" against the modern fighter. The bomber would *not* always get through, certainly not in daylight. Surely the Trenchard philosophy must now be dead and buried alongside the bodies of so many young aircrew?

Not so. There was to be no rethink on specification B.1/39, issued to create the daddy of all heavily armed bombers, the Lancaster. The Halifax had just made its maiden flight, even now not too late to cancel. But that too would go ahead. And Ludlow-Hewitt must be made to pay for being so accurate in his prediction. He was sacked to be replaced by Charles Portal, another Trenchard man, through and through. The "sluggers" were not beaten yet.

Fortunately for de Havilland, Freeman still had a mind of his own. In a meeting in November, he agreed with de Havilland that there must be some form of alternative bomber. In December, they put their case to a committee that included the Assistant Chief of Air Staff, the Commander in Chief, Bomber Command, and others. It took a great deal of persuasion to overcome their understandable reservations over something that was, at that time, no more than a model aeroplane, hanging from the ceiling of a kitchen in an old manor house. De Havilland promised them a 1,500 lb bomb load over 1,500 miles at a cruising speed of 320 mph and a maximum speed of 404 mph. Partially convinced by men with a proven track record, they gave their grudging assent to an order for 50 planes as reconnaissance aircraft. They still could not bring themselves to go that extra mile and see it as a bomber. By Christmas, 1939, specification B.1/40 was drawn up and delivered to Hatfield in January 1940. Roy Chadwick at Avro, with his B.1/39, had been given almost a year's start but the race was on.

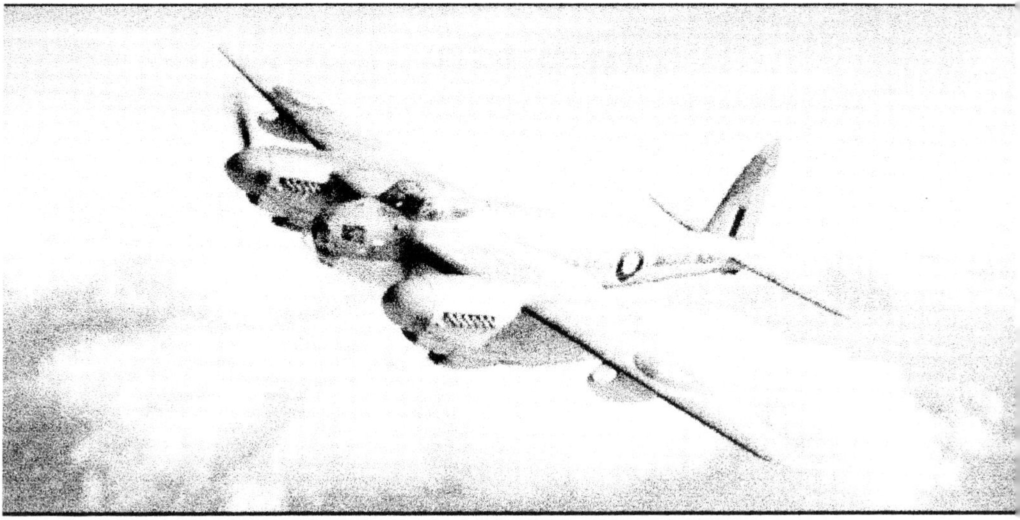

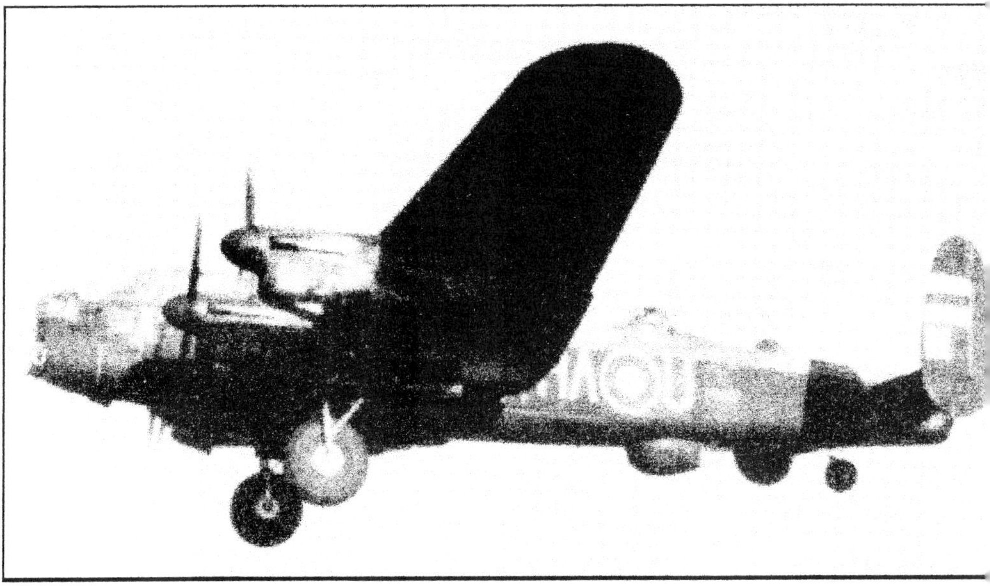

Chapter Nine

While the order for 50 Mosquitos spurred on the team at Salisbury Hall, it also brought its problems. Ministry "brass hats" began to appear, only too keen to have a finger in the pie. Their main contribution was a demand that a gunner should be installed in a turret immediately behind the pilot and bomb aimer. Much time was wasted, trying to explain how this would defeat the whole object of the design but there was much shaking of official heads. Who had ever heard of a bomber without a machine gun aboard? The men from Whitehall also complained, with rather more justification, about the projected bomb load, four 250 lbs. This was solved by reducing to a minimum the size of the bombs' fins - the team bombed their own airfield to test the new design - and, overnight, the bomb load was doubled and the critics silenced once more.

During the bitter winter months of early 1940, as the BEF was frozen in its "phoney war" and the RAF had to be content with dropping propaganda leaflets over Germany at night, progress at Salisbury Hall was steady and uninterrupted. But with the spring came events that threatened the whole venture once again. Germany invaded the Low Countries and Churchill was swept to power by back-benchers disenchanted with Chamberlain as a war leader. Then came the evacuation of the BEF from Dunkirk, then the preparation for the Battle of Britain that all knew must follow. One of Churchill's first actions was to appoint Lord Beaverbrook as the first Minister for Aircraft Production; one of Beaverbrook's first actions to cancel the order for the Mosquito and instruct de Havillands to convert to repairing Hurricane fighters. But Beaverbrook had underestimated Freeman's powers of persuasion even without the threat of the tommy gun which Freeman, in common with all Whitehall staff, kept in his office in readiness for any hand to hand fighting required to combat the invading German hordes. By July, thanks to Freeman, production of the Mosquito

The Trenchard Touch

began again. At the height of the Battle of Britain, Freeman even managed to "scrounge" two Rolls Royce Merlins for the prototype.

The plane's wooden construction, essentially balsa sandwiched between two layers of birch, stuck together with glue, presented few problems and several advantages. It meant the plane could be built in two halves, split longitudinally, making cockpit and control installation simple before the two halves were stuck together. Skilled metal fitters and turners were in short supply, woodworkers readily available and a well dispersed "cottage industry" sprang up around Hatfield as the prototype approached completion. A local furniture firm, G-plan, with its specialised knowledge of synthetic resins and glues, became heavily involved. Finally, on November 3, less than a month after the de Havilland factory had taken direct hits from a low flying JU88, disassembled and heavily disguised, the prototype left Salisbury Hall by road for Hatfield. The same day, their staunch friend, Freeman, much against his will, was promoted to Vice Chief of the Air Staff under Charles Portal. While now wielding much more "clout", he was to miss his involvement in technical problems but at least he took with him the satisfaction of knowing he had saved the Mosquito from extinction.

On November 24, taxiing trials were successfully carried out. The next day, a mere 11 months after its initial order, prototype W4050, the first of the Mosquitos, flew. At the controls was de Havilland's eldest son, also Geoffrey, the baby who had flown, cradled in his mother's arms, in his father's first plane. John Walker, head of the Engine Installation Department, sat alongside him. The Mosquito's maiden flight lasted almost three quarters of an hour, far in excess of the usual first flight. It had performed immaculately, climbing to 15,000 feet with ease. Back on the ground, Geoffrey reported "all well" to his father, surrounded by a delighted group of de Havilland faithful including Alan Butler.

Intricate test flying followed as each system was thoroughly checked. Then came the ultimate test - how fast was it? Air speed indicators tended to be inaccurate. The answer was to "borrow" one of the latest Spitfires, the fastest current British plane, and race against it. Side by side in level flight, the Mosquito outpaced the Spitfire by at least 20 mph. At 30,000 feet it reached 425 mph. For the next two-and-a-half years, no other plane in the world would be able to catch the Mosquito in level flight.

So - de Havilland had the fastest plane in the world, faster than anything R.J. Mitchell had ever built. Now he must "sell" it, first to the Air Force and then to the politicians. There had been a change of political leadership. The question was; had it heralded a change in their attitude to strategic bombing?

When the Germans invaded the Channel Islands in 1940, not everyone was sad to see them arrive. Edward Chapman was in jail. Jersey's occupation meant his liberation. Eddie Chapman was a colourful character. There was nothing vicious in his make-up. He simply enjoyed excitement.

As a young man in Sunderland he had been awarded a certificate for bravery by the Humane Society for saving a man from drowning. In the nineteen thirties he had served his King and Country loyally as a Coldstream Guardsman and, finding life rather dull after his honourable discharge, had taken up a new profession, that of safe-cracking. He had proved to have a gift for the profession and he had prospered. Unfortunately for him, in 1939 he had been discovered by the police, redhanded, applying his expertise to a safe in Glasgow.

Arrested and incarcerated, he had not gone to trial, having escaped from jail and made his way to Jersey. There he had been arrested once more and had been on the point of being returned to Glasgow when the Germans had ridden to his rescue.

The Germans found to their delight that they had in their grasp a brave, disciplined ex-soldier, English speaking and an expert safe-cracker, experienced in handling explosives. They made him an offer he could not refuse, taking into consideration the alternatives described. Promised excitement galore, Eddie was sent for "training".

In 1917, when Minister of Munitions, Churchill had written, "It is improbable that any terrorisation of the civil population which could be achieved by air attack would compel the Government of a nation to surrender." Now he was Prime Minister. Had his opinion changed? De Havilland had no illusion regarding his aeroplane. It was no instrument of mass destruction. And that would not have worried him. His main anxiety was whether this high speed bomber, perfect in design for precision, tactical bombing, would find a role in whatever the politicians and the RAF "top brass" had in mind. Had he any right to be hopeful, having in mind Churchill's stated opinion during the last war?

In August, as Goering foolishly diverted his bombers away from the fighter stations in the south, bombs began to fall on London. The country demanded retaliation and 81 twin-engined bombers were despatched by night to bring retribution to the German capital. Only 29 claimed even to have reached the city, no significant damage was done and eight planes were lost in the process; eight crews sacrificed so that Britain could wake up to morale boosting newspaper headlines, "Berlin Bombed". It was hardly surprising then, considering the miserable performance of his front line bombers over Berlin, that Portal should announce that their long-term strategy would be based on the four engined bomber.

But the Stirling was only just beginning to come into squadron service to replace the Wellington. The delivery of the first Halifax was still months away. Neither plane looked like being a world beater. That left the Lancaster. But the prototype had yet to fly, beaten into the air by months by the Mosquito despite having had nearly a year's start. Was this an indication of the plane's complexity and the number of man-hours it would be required to make one? A great deal would be expected from the Lancaster if it was going to make good the politicians' bravado for, not for the first time in his career, Churchill had changed his mind.

On July 8, Churchill wrote, "There is one thing that will bring Hitler down, and that is an absolutely devastating, exterminating attack by very heavy bombers from this country upon the Nazi homeland. We must be able to overwhelm them by this means, without which I do not see a way through." And, if that was insufficiently clear, in a September memorandum, he stated, "The Navy can lose us the war but only the Air Force can win it. The fighters are our salvation but the bombers alone provide the means of victory. The Air Force and its action on the largest scale must therefore ... claim first place over the Army or the Navy," going on to cast doubt on the likely effect of precision attacks on such targets as oil refineries.

In October, Churchill wrote to his Air Minister, Sir Archibald Sinclair, asking, "that a wholehearted effort shall be made to cart a large number of bombs into Germany, under conditions in which admittedly no special accuracy could be obtained." To his credit, Sinclair had the temerity to stand up to the great man, arguing that even a small bomber force, by accurate bombing, would do very great damage to the enemy's war effort, but could not gain a decision against Germany by bombing the civil population. But Churchill had dominated stronger men than Sinclair who, deciding he could not beat them, joined them, becoming an enthusiastic member of the small select group which dominated strategic policy. Within days, the Cabinet had agreed that "The civilian population around the target area must be made to feel the weight of the war."

Indicative of the Prime Minister's aggressive attitude was his treatment of Hugh Dowding, Britain's saviour at the Battle of Britain no more than a few weeks previously. Though he claimed it "broke his heart" to do so, he agreed with Portal that Dowding was too defensively minded, relieving him of his command and packing him off as Head of the British Air Commission in Washington. *Sic transit gloria.* Churchill rounded off the year with a memo to his Secretary of State for Air, the Chief of the Air Staff and the Minister for Aircraft Production. "I consider the rapid expansion of the bomber force one of the greatest military objectives now before us."

Allowances must be made for Churchill's *volte face*. Britain, valiantly supported by her Commonwealth, stood alone, the only country still at war with Hitler. Bombing was the only way he could see of taking the war to the enemy. The alternative was unthinkable. But what future did a small, sleek bomber have in such a quest for sheer indiscriminate destruction?

With the impetus of Churchill's tireless energy behind it, a plan was drawn up for a bomber force of 4,000 front line four engined heavies, this at a time when a mere 500 of all varieties could be mustered. The Halifax was proving to require 76,000 man-hours to complete one aircraft. The Lancaster was likely to take more. Four or five Mosquitos could be produced in that time. Needing two engines instead of four, no armament to install, two crew only to train rather than seven, was there no one who could put the argument to the policy makers? As late as August and September, letters and memos were still flashing between Chadwick at Avro, the Royal Aircraft Establishment, the Director of Technical Development at the Ministry of Aircraft Production and the Principal Technical Officer to the Air Council, as doubts lingered over the complexity and expense of the Lancaster. It was argued again that perhaps a modified Manchester might still be a better, cheaper option. It was even suggested that Chadwick should be instructed to make the Halifax, a plane he held in low regard. Finally the contract for the first prototype Lancaster was granted, but with misgivings. Yet, such was the accepted mental image of the perfect bomber - four engined, bristling with turrets and guns, crammed full of expendable youth - that the Mosquito never entered the picture.

Against this background, de Havilland arranged the first official demonstration of the Mosquito's capabilities. On April 20, 1941, not many weeks after the first flight of the Lancaster prototype, Geoffrey de Havilland put the plane through its paces in front of Beaverbrook, Freeman, General Arnold of the USAAF and a gaggle of lesser ministry "brass hats", some of whom had been amongst those who had claimed there was no time to design a revolutionary plane for *this* war. In the circumstances, de Havilland could be excused a little theatre. Before the Mosquito flew, he arranged a fly past of a series of lumbering aircraft, including several American Lend-Lease, to set the scene. Then came the Mosquito, hurtling low over the field at close to 400 mph. The contrast was electrifying. There followed an aerobatic display including a series of upward rolls and it took a little time for the audience to realise they were all being performed with one propeller feathered.

The impact was immediate. General Arnold was particularly impressed, returning home to the USA a few days later with a full set of Mosquito drawings. But the demonstration of the Mosquito's speed also proved a drawback. To the official mind, such speed was wasted on a bomber. If it flew faster than a Spitfire then it had to be a fighter; if not a fighter then at least a fighter-bomber; or pure reconnaissance, perhaps. The fact that the installation of four 20 mm cannon and four machine guns in the nose immediately reduced its speed dramatically made no impression and, in order to ensure the steady stream of orders that now came in, de Havilland was obliged to accept that only a small proportion of his aircraft would be made, as designed, as high speed bombers. He even had to fight off a demand from the Admiralty who saw in the Mosquito the ideal target tower. And someone was even crazy enough to suggest not one but two turrets. In the end, de Havilland had to accept that, of the initial 150 now ordered, most would be equipped as fighter bombers, a few as reconnaissance planes and no more than a small residue as pure bombers.

Full production of the Mosquito began, centred at Hatfield but with well dispersed sub-contractors scattered around. The second completed Mosquito however was still at Salisbury Hall. To save dismantling and reassembling it if transported by road, Geoffrey decided to fly it out from an adjoining field. A small portion of hedge was removed for that purpose. On May 13, two days before the Mosquito took off, something else landed nearby, gliding silently out of the night sky. Suspended from his parachute was SS Obersturmführer Karl Richard Richter. Undetected, he buried all evidence of his arrival, along with a stock of food and a radio transmitter. He went to earth in a nearby wood, not venturing forth until after dark on the 14th. Within minutes of striding out in his camel hair coat and trilby hat, a lorry driver, lost in the blackout, stopped to ask the way only to be met with a stream of arrogant abuse in a thick foreign accent. The lorry driver told his story at the next police station and, in quick time, War Reserve Police Constable A.J. Scott made the arrest of his life to send Richter ultimately to his death in Wandsworth Prison.

The factory had already been the victim of a precision bombing attack by a JU88 and now a spy had been caught within a mile of Hatfield. Had the Mosquito's reputation already spread that far?

During the latter months of 1940, both the RAF and the Luftwaffe were taught a lesson in mass aerial attacks at night. They differed only in that the Luftwaffe learned from it, the RAF did not. From September 7 to November 2, London was bombed every night - the so-called London Blitz. But the German aircraft, already becoming obsolescent with no new designs to replace them, had been designed essentially for Army co-operation, not to bomb cities in the dead of night. Neither had their crews been trained for such attacks. Their destruction in London was ill-defined, not intentionally - the British Bomber Command would be the only air force specifically programmed to terrorise the populace - but on account of being given targets no more pin-point than the vague dockland area. In the early months of 1941, unimpressed with their results, they switched to industrial areas, their last sustained night attack being on Birmingham in May. From then on, German air raids would become sporadic nuisances, nothing more. In the most major of their attacks they had dropped no more than 100 tons, trivial when compared with the weight of bombs to be dropped nightly by the RAF in years to come, and throughout their accuracy had been lamentable, even when they had begun navigating along a radio beam. It was even claimed later that Dublin had been bombed on one occasion in mistake for Belfast.

But their bombing campaign had always been inaccurate rather than indiscriminate though the civil population who suffered and died around the industrial areas would have been hard put to recognise the distinction. Death and terror are death and terror whether the intention is there or not but, somehow, life went on. In a panic stampede in Bethnal Green underground shelter, 173 men, women and children were crushed to death but there was no mass rioting; the Government was not brought down. And it was ironic that the country that gave the world the word *Blitzkrieg* was the first to recognise the futility of trying to bomb a nation into submission.

Was there any evidence that Britain could succeed where Germany had failed? Was there any evidence to suggest that the RAF, also never really trained for night attack, was faring any better?

American observers in Germany were already sceptical when matching the RAF's claims against what they saw on the ground. However, it was an independent report by a member of the Cabinet secretariat, commissioned by Lindemann, Churchill's scientific adviser, now Lord Cherwell, that put hard figures to over-enthusiastic rough estimates. The Butt report in August 1941 was damning. Of the 67 per cent of planes launched which had claimed to have attacked the target, only 20 per cent had dropped their bombs within five miles. In the Ruhr, where the defences were particularly strong, only seven per cent had bombed within five miles. Only one in 15 crews had come within five miles of the target on a moonless night. 40,000 of the 54,000 tons of bombs dropped had done so in open countryside. The Stirlings and Halifaxes, carrying their five tons of bombs at 200 mph, had been losing one plane for every 10 tons of bombs dropped. The Halifax tended to spin uncontrollably when fully loaded or go into an inverted dive from rudder stalling. Half as many were being lost in training and testing as on operations.

It was understandable then that Churchill, having read such damning evidence, began to hedge his bets. While still committed to the plan for 4,000 heavy bombers, he wrote to Portal, "It is very disputable whether bombing by itself will be a decisive factor in the present war. On the contrary, all that we learnt since the war began shows that its effects, both physical and moral, are greatly exaggerated." That was in August. By October, he had shifted his position even further. Again, writing to the Chief of the Air Staff, he wrote, "I deprecate however placing unbounded confidence in this form of attack and still more in expressing that confidence in terms of mathematics. Even if all the towns of Germany were rendered largely uninhabitable, it does not follow that the military control would be weakened or even that war industry would not be carried on. A different picture would be presented if the enemy's Air Force was so far reduced as to enable heavy accurate daylight bombing of factories to take place. This however cannot be done outside the radius of fighter protection, according to what I am at present told." At the turn of the year, Churchill pointed out that, in 1941, while 1900 aircraft had been total losses due to enemy action, 2,500 had been lost in flying accidents, demanding, "... you make me proposals for effecting a substantial reduction." It was becoming apparent that Bomber Command's current campaign was killing more young Britons than Germans and, in November, it was called off.

It is a matter of conjecture what might have resulted if Churchill, in this mood, had been influenced by someone who might have convinced him that there *was* another kind of bomber, there was another method of attack, that specific targets in Germany *could* be attacked, accurately, in daylight, without fighter escort. Where was Beaverbrook or, for that matter Freeman, both of whom had witnessed what a Mosquito could do? The fact that Freeman was also a strong supporter of Avro's Chadwick and his Lancaster need not have precluded him from pressing the Mosquito's case. There was already some evidence that could have been put before the all powerful man. In mid-September, Mosquitos of No.1 Photographic Reconnaissance Unit had flown operationally, a full month before the first flight of a production Lancaster. On its first operation, photographing harbours from 4.5 miles high, a Mosquito had left three ME109s, sent to intercept, trailing below in its wake.

But it wasn't to be. By the end of 1941, with the promise of Lancasters in 1942, it was back to more of the same. The way had been prepared by an Air Staff Paper in September. "The ultimate aim of an attack on a town area," it laid down, "is to break the morale of the population which occupies it. To ensure this we must achieve two things; first we must make the town physically uninhabitable and, secondly, we must make the people conscious of constant personal danger. The immediate aim is, therefore, twofold, namely, to produce (i) destruction and (ii) the fear of death."

A city was still about as precise a target that could be identified by night and, in February 1942, in Air Ministry Directive S.463668/111 Portal made it clear that "... the aiming points are to be the built-up areas, not, for instance, the dockyards or aircraft factories." He sought to bring to a very inaccurate science, the beauty of mathematics, something of which Churchill had already disapproved. The scale of attack, the directive stated, was to be one ton per 800 population. Cities were listed as primary or alternative targets. Losing a home had been found the most demoralising effect of German raids over Britain and, accordingly, Lord Cherwell went further in applying mathematics in an effort to lend dignity to a ghastly illusion. One ton of bombs, dropped on a built-up area, he claimed, based on a study of the effects of German bombing in Britain, would destroy 20 to 40 homes, rendering 100 to 200 homeless. One bomber, he estimated, surviving 14 missions, would deliver 40 tons of bombs in its life, therefore making between 4,000 and 8,000 homeless. He deduced from that that 10,000 bombers, attacking 58 cities, would render one-third of the German population homeless. Both Portal and Secretary of State Sinclair found Cherwell's figures "simple, clear and convincing."

Their only problem remaining was where were they to find a commander, another Trenchard, with the mental attributes to successfully prosecute such a campaign? They decided that Arthur Harris, he of the North West Frontier, would fill the bill admirably. On February 22, 1942, Arthur "Bomber" Harris was created Commander in Chief of Bomber Command.

On the same day that Harris took command, A.V. Hill, Member of Parliament for Cambridge University, speaking in the House of Commons, declared, "The idea of bombing a well defended enemy into submission or severely affecting his morale - or even doing substantial damage to him - is an illusion." But a few words from one of the most brilliant thinkers in the country - he had been involved from the start in the development of Radar - stood no chance of stopping an aerial Juggernaut with a man in control straight out of the Haig-Trenchard mould.

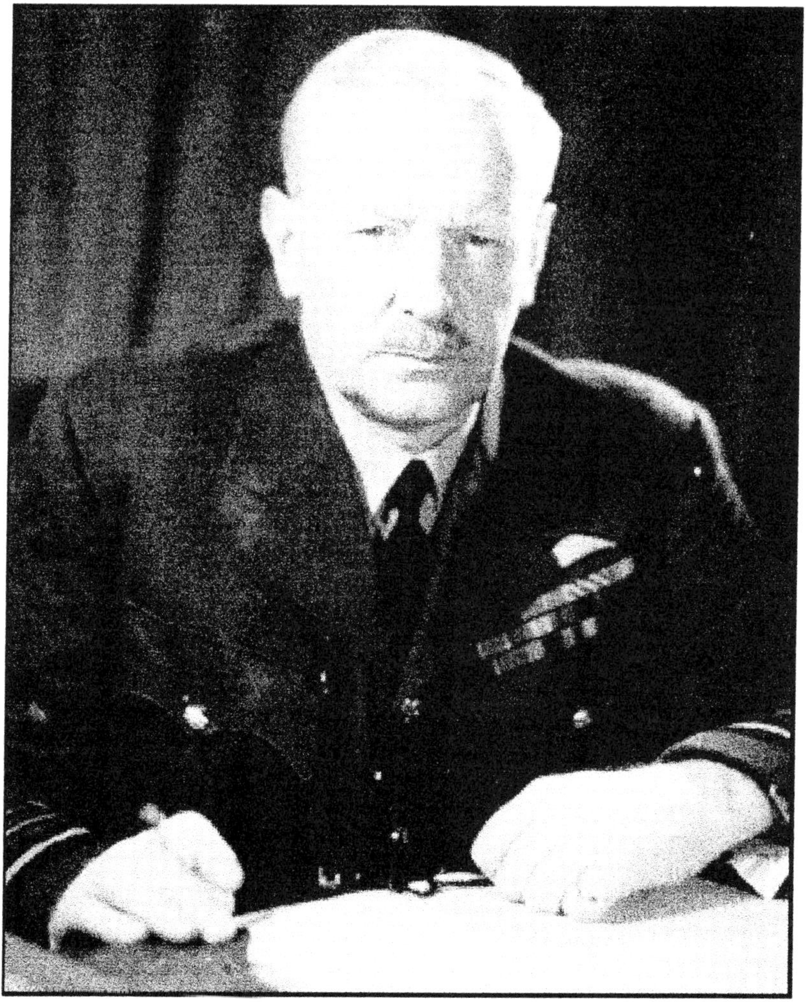

Chapter Ten

And so, it began. Knowing the man, no one would have expected Harris to ease himself quietly into the job. His last operational experience had been bombing defenceless rebel tribesmen into submission. How much of that attitude of mind still lingered? In February 1942, he took over a dispirited force equipped with some 400 operational aircraft, about one-third of which were heavies; Stirlings and Halifaxes. In March, the first Lancaster operational sortie took place, mine laying. Barely a month later, on April 17, Harris decided to signal his arrival to the enemy, demonstrating at the same time the power of the new bomber in a low level, daylight raid deep into Germany. Those disastrous daylight raids back in 1939, they had been in Blenheims and Wellingtons. This was to be the Lancaster; quite a different matter. To ensure the raid's success, Harris ordered that the most experienced crews available should take part - no longer an easy task. With 7,448 aircrew already killed, most of the pre-war professional flyers were now dead, prisoners of war or promoted.

The target was to be the U-boat diesel engine plant at Augsburg in Bavaria, not even included in the Minister for Economic Warfare, Lord Selbourne's priority list. Targets of greater strategic importance, reached over shorter, less well defended distances, were scorned. Twelve planes would take part.

Of the 12, four were shot down on the way to the target, their armament no defence against determined fighter attacks with 20 mm cannon. Three more fell over the target. The five on the return flight, lighter and faster, survived. Seventeen bombs had hit the target, only twelve exploding. It was 1918, Trenchard and 99 Squadron, all over again as if nothing had changed. Fifty experienced crew had been sacrificed to a man's ego. It was a miracle that Harris was not sacked. No Admiral or General would have survived a comparable disaster.

But at least the raid had proved one thing. With Germany's air defence as it was, the Lancaster, though designed specifically for that purpose, could not operate in daylight. It must be switched, along with all the other heavies, to night attack. But would it fare any better in this role than its predecessors? It was faster, to be sure, but would its heavy defensive armaments prove any greater protection at night? There had been a saying in the 1914-18 war: "you never hear the shell that hits you." In the darkness, the bomber rarely saw the fighter that shot it down, never the flak shell to which the low altitude and speed of a cumbersome mass made it so vulnerable.

Completely unabashed, in true Trenchard tradition, Harris determined to demonstrate the power of night attack. Late in May, putting into the air every serviceable aircraft he could find, including some borrowed from Coastal Command, the famous first thousand bomber raid took place. There was no hypocritical nonsense about industrial or military targets. The target had been simply Cologne. And the British public loved it. Their ecstatic reaction to the first true terror attack encouraged the politicians to give Harris virtual *carte blanche* for the campaign to come. Churchill went along with the flow, modifying his attitude yet again. "It would be a mistake," he wrote in a Memo reviewing the war position, "to cast aside our original thought, namely, that the severe, ruthless bombing of Germany on an ever increasing scale will not cripple her war effort but will also create conditions intolerable to the mass of the German population."

The Cologne raid had opened the floodgates for what was to come but it had also yielded indirectly one other vital piece of information. The next morning, a Mosquito, sent to reconnoitre the city in daylight, flew low and fast over the roof tops, gleaming with the highly polished fuselage that had been shown to increase speed by as much as 10 mph. The man in the street below was clearly visible. Surprised, the crew noted that no one looked up. It took a little while for them to realise that at that height, at that speed and with the sibilance of aerodynamic near perfection, their approach had been as near silent as made no difference. Just as in the case of the 1914-18 shell with "your name on it," had the Mosquito been on a bombing run, those down below would not have known what had hit them.

Harris resembled Trenchard in ways other than their tunnel vision of aerial warfare. "A bomber offensive weight," he declared, "if continued for long enough, would be something that no country in the world would endure." He also, with his undoubted powers of leadership, was to engender an extraordinary degree of hero worship amongst the aircrew who, night after night, would give their lives in his pursuit of the impossible. His prickly, bluff, bellicose personality would result in a popularity with the British people that would save him from being sacked as losses began to be unacceptable. It also blinded them to the cost, both in terms of their sons and the diversion of precious resources away from the Army and the Navy. He would even have as his Deputy Commander in Chief a gentle man, resembling in many ways Maurice Baring. Robert Saundby, responsible for day to day operational matters, for ensuring that his chief's instructions were fully understood down to squadron level, was a sensitive and cultured man. He differed from Baring only in that he was totally in awe of his chief, no doubt happiest when able to escape from Harris's overpowering aura to indulge his passions for fly fishing and butterfly collecting. Harris, like Trenchard, made enemies of anyone who did not agree with him. The choice of an affable, malleable man as his second in command could not have been more favourable for him as he set about his task.

Harris, like Trenchard, also saw no logic in resting crews while reserves were built up. Fear that inactivity in the air might strengthen the demands of the Army and Navy spurred him on. Throughout 1942, night after night, so long as the weather permitted, attacks were kept up with no real focus other than area bombing of one German city after another. The unpredictability of the attacks had one fringe benefit in that, while ineffective in terms of damage either to industry or morale, it tied down thousands of men in the defence of Germany when they could have been better employed elsewhere. Early in 1943, the Ruhr came in for particularly close attention. After over 18,000 sorties flown against it, there was still nothing to suggest cracks in civilian morale and it occurred to Harris and his staff that perhaps they were going about it the wrong way.

Photographic evidence was accumulating, along with that gained during the London Blitz, that fire was far more destructive than high explosive. A factory with its roof caved in, its windows blown out, was capable of repair. German engineers had become masters of the art of shielding their machinery from conventional explosives. Fire on the other hand, raging through a plant, destroyed completely everything in its path. But fire needs oxygen. It was simple logic then to first blow out the windows and blow off the roof, before the main incendiary attack. Where better to try out the theory than with Lübeck and Rostock with their old wooden houses? Encouraged with the result, another preliminary raid on Krefeld in what was now to be called Operation Gomorrah was also voted a success. It was time for Harris to look elsewhere for a more ambitious target. He chose Hamburg, not for any particular strategic reason. Admittedly Hamburg was a major port but that would be no more than a convenient excuse for what he had in mind. And Hamburg, unlike Augsburg, was within easy reach over the sea and readily identifiable on H2S, the current navigational aid. The fire raids on Hamburg killed 40,000 people and made a million more homeless. The heart of the fires created giant anticlockwise vortices over the city, up to five km high and three km in diameter. The air sucked in at their bases created winds of hurricane force. Flames roared along streets faster than a man could run. Women and children were roasted or suffocated where they cowered in bunker or cellar. The attacks were only called off when exhausted crews could find nothing more in the centre of the city worth bombing. The fire raids on Hamburg were the quintessence of terror bombing, carried out at a time when, to the British populace at large, "the only good German was a dead German." The daily news of the havoc being wreaked on German cities was received, if not with jubilation, with quiet satisfaction. Even so, there were a few brave souls that spoke out against it. The Marquess of Salisbury, in a letter to Sinclair, the Secretary of State, feared that they were losing the moral superiority to the Germans while Captain Basil Liddel Hart, a distinguished and respected military thinker, opposed the campaign throughout. Their puny efforts might have stood a chance of exerting some influence had they received the backing of the Church. Dr George Bell, Bishop of Chichester, a saintly man actively involved pre-war in aiding Jews to escape the Nazi regime, incurred Churchill's wrath in his outspoken criticism of the bombing strategy but most churchmen approved the campaign. "Frequently," wrote Dr Garbett, Archbishop of York, "the choice has to be made between the lesser of two evils and it is the lesser of two evils to bomb a war-loving Germany than to sacrifice the lives of our fellow countrymen who long for peace and to delay delivering millions now held in slavery." In 1940, the German raid on Coventry had destroyed 100 acres out of 1,922. In Hamburg 6,200 acres out of 8,382 were razed to the ground. And yet, within weeks of the RAF switching their attacks elsewhere - what they had done to Hamburg they thought they could do to Berlin - survivors were already creeping back into the ruins.

Life went on.

Eddie Chapman was ready. His Abwehr controllers were happy that his training was complete. His parachute jumps at night must have tested his appetite for excitement but they had been concluded to the instructor's satisfaction. His knowledge of explosives had required broadening. It is one thing to handle the amounts required to blow a safe, another to destroy an aircraft factory. But, cheerfully confident, Eddie had pleased his new masters, not only with his adaptability but with his ardent conversion to National Socialism. Always the most amicable of characters, he had, while employed at the centre of German Military Intelligence, made friends, had taken time to study their ways.

On the night of December 20, 1942, given the codename Fritschen, as fully equipped as any self-respecting agent should be with radio, pistol, £1,000 and a suicide pill, he landed by parachute near Ely. His mission? To blow up the de Havilland aircraft factory at Hatfield with a bonus of £15,000 and a ticket to the USA if he was successful.

Fortunately or unfortunately - with Eddie it would forever be somewhat uncertain which word truly applied - Bletchley Park had been monitoring the Abwehr's instructions to their agent and Eddie's arrival was not altogether unexpected. Whether Eddie was aware of this or not is another mystery but what is certain is that Eddie's first difficulty after landing was convincing the local police that he was a German spy who now wished to work as a double agent. Finally persuaded to give MI5 a ring, Eddie's identity was confirmed and he was swept into the welcoming arms of the British Secret Service.

MI5 did not fancy the codename, Fritschen, and gave him one of their own, Zig Zag. But first he must be allowed to radio the Abwehr to confirm his safe arrival. Then a convincing destruction of the factory at Hatfield had to be arranged. MI5 stood and watched as Eddie, carrying out the first stage of his original plan, acquired his explosives from a quarry in Stevenage, a source he had found invaluable in his days as a safecracker. In January, in the dead of night, he and an MI5 officer scaled the boundary fence around the factory, planting their "bombs" at strategic points. A famous illusionist, rejoicing in the name of Jasper Maskelyne, then, with a controlled explosion and much smoke, blew off a section of the roof, scattering spare machinery parts around the factory floor to complete the illusion.

The damage was reported in all the national newspapers in terms that suggested the damage caused had been far greater than that admitted, and Eddie received a message of congratulations from his controllers in Berlin. He was instructed to make his way back to Germany where they would honour their pledge of £15,000 and the trip to the USA, on the strict understanding that he would undertake similar acts of sabotage there also. MI5 put him on a British boat, bound for Lisbon, hoping to keep a check on him in America.

But Eddie had a request to make of MI5 before he boarded his boat. He would like very much, with their help, to assassinate Hitler.

And, while Harris continued to plough his straight, narrow furrow,

The Trenchard Touch

what of the Mosquito bomber? How had it fared while all public attention had been focused on death and destruction? Harris made no secret of the fact that he had no time for the plane. The fact that, while still remaining the fastest plane in the world, it now carried a 4,000 lb. bomb load, equal to the maximum a Flying Fortress ever managed, still failed to impress the Commander in Chief. As a fighter bomber, like all such planes, neither fish nor fowl, it had not succeeded though it was already staking its claim as the finest of night fighters, with two kills within 10 minutes on its first successful sortie. And, of course, as a reconnaissance aircraft it was peerless.

But what of the Mosquito bomber, the aircraft it was designed to be? In truth, its early days were far from auspicious, due almost entirely to lack of numbers and command enthusiasm. In July 1942, there were but two Mosquito bomber squadrons, No. 105 and No. 139. One problem was that though aircrew had been posted to 139, they did not have any planes to fly; 105 possessed but eight. Such was the attitude to the Mosquito in the shade of the Lancaster. Indifferent results from their early operations, during which they lost a station commander and a squadron leader, also did not help their cause and the Mosquito bomber came close to abandonment at that stage. The only person who seemed genuinely impressed was Herman Goering who ranted at his designers for not providing him with anything that could catch it in flight. But Goering must have had a short memory. On August 27, 1939, days only before the outbreak of war, the He 178 had flown for the first time. The brain-child of the son of a Berlin light bulb distributor, Hans Joachim Pabst von Ohain, a brilliant physicist who, after the war, would become the Director of the US Airforce Aeronautical Research Laboratory, it had been powered by a jet engine. Frank Whittle's Gloster prototype E29/39 would not fly until May 1941.

Both Hitler and Goering had seen the He178 perform and, as they had not expected a prolonged war, had seen little purpose in pursuing any plan for a plane that would fly faster than sound. After three flights, the He178 had been abandoned. Years ahead of its time, if successfully developed, it would have been more than a match for the Mosquito, catastrophic for the Lancaster.

What ultimately saved the Mosquito bomber was a raid in September 1942, carried out on the Gestapo HQ in Oslo where a high level Nazi rally was being held. Four planes attacked at low level and, while the total of death and destruction might have been unremarkable, an article in the *Daily Express* made the British public aware for the first time of a new bomber they possessed. To a populace satiated with accounts of carpet bombing and becoming more and more disillusioned with the official lip-service paid to military targets, - Clement Attlee, the Deputy Prime Minister had vehemently denied in the House of Commons that there was any indiscriminate bombing - the mental picture of high speed, low level aircraft, delivering their bombs within 50 to 100 yards of the target in broad daylight was like a breath of fresh air.

Prompted by their success in Oslo, targeting groups of high ranking officers became a speciality. Similar highly productive raids were carried out on Gestapo HQs, one in the Aarhus University buildings when one plane returned to base with a piece of masonry embedded in its fuselage, and another at Shell House in Copenhagen. Some latitude was permitted in the latter raid as the only building alongside the Gestapo HQ likely to be damaged was a brothel frequented by the staff officers.

The sheer ability of the Mosquito bomber now drove it to the top, even against the dead weight of Harris's disapproval. Harris had done all he could to obstruct the formation of the Pathfinder squadrons, arguing that they would simply denude the rank and file squadrons of their best crews. It required Portal, with the backing of the War Cabinet, to pluck up the courage to overrule him. At first, it was routine for Pathfinder Lancasters to mark the target area for the main stream heavies. By December 1942 however, Mosquitos were marking the target for the Pathfinder Lancasters which, in turn, guided the main stream. Their cabins were now pressurised, giving them a ceiling of over 37,000 feet where they could roam at will, virtually unassailable. Now capable of 437 mph in level flight at 29,000 feet, they flew too high and too fast to be concerned with anything the Germans could throw at them in the form of fighter or flak.

But away from the Pathfinders, the Mosquitos had perfected a technique of bombing in a shallow dive from 2,000 feet, giving them an average bombing error of 60 yards. First, low level planes dropped their bombs with 11 second fuses from about 50 feet, the second attack being made in a shallow dive from 2,000 feet with instantaneous fuses. Accurate timing was required if the last Mosquito was not going to be brought down by the explosions on the ground but the damage caused by this combination was as devastating as it was accurate. Anxious to prove the technique in combat, a daylight raid on the Schneider plant at Le Creusot proved highly successful, losing only one plane out of 94. It finally tipped the scales in the Mosquito's favour. As if to drive home the point, another daylight raid in December on the Phillips works at Eindhoven was so accurate as to prompt the Dutch Minister in London to express the gratitude of the Dutch people at the minimal loss of civilian life that had resulted.

This all coincided with Wilfrid Freeman being appointed Chief Executive at the Ministry of Aircraft Production and a demonstration of the Mosquito in Washington that had the Americans raving about it. General Arnold, already a convert, begged for 250, offering Mustangs in exchange. Colonel Elliot Roosevelt, the President's son, had already used his influence to acquire one in North Africa and swore by it. Later, he would replace the Lightnings of the whole of the reconnaissance wing of the 8th USAAF with Mosquitos.

In January 1943 came the defining moment. Mosquitos raided Berlin in daylight, not once in the day but twice, their attacks timed to coincide with Goering's broadcast to the German people as part of the celebration of the tenth anniversary of Hitler's rise to power. The Wehrmacht top brass were invited to the Hall of Honour at the Reich Air Ministry to hear the Reichmarshal speak. But Berlin radio suddenly went off the air as three of 105 Squadron's most experienced crews sped over the city at 350 mph, dropping their bombs to return unscathed. Goebbels, speaking some hours later was similarly interrupted though at the loss of one Mosquito.

Finally converted by such audacity, Harris became a devotee, demanding more and more Mosquito bombers. Now everyone, the Americans included, wanted them and production, outstripping Hatfield's capacity, spread to Canada with its vast timber reserves. Packard in America would, under licence, provide the Merlins.

But would Bomber Harris have the imagination, the power of alternative thinking, to make the best out of this new found weapon? Crews trained in the specialised art of low level daylight bombing were already fretting in their Pathfinder duties. Was he to remain blind to the plane's true potential?

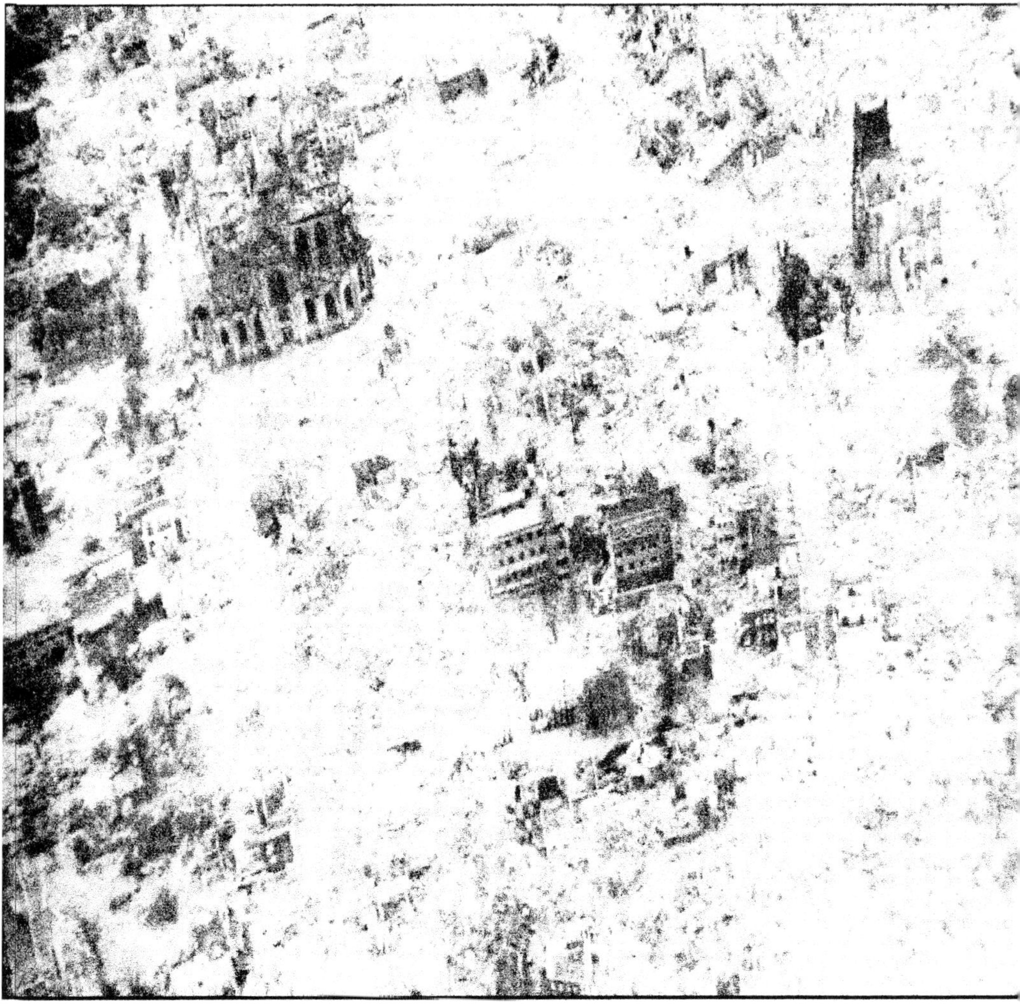

Chapter Eleven

Albert Speer could hardly have been described as standing apart from the Nazi leadership. But, in many ways, he differed from the rest of the political gangsters who ruled the greater part of Europe at that time. Undoubtedly, he was intelligent, but then, within the realms of their perversion, so were Hitler, Goebbels, Himmler and Heydrich. But Albert Speer would probably have risen to international fame in his profession whoever had been in power. That he developed a facultative blindness to the activities of his colleagues, including the deaths of his slave labourers, was his shame but he was the only Nazi leader known to have been deeply affected by the fire bombing of Hamburg, not by the industrial damage, which was insignificant, but by the human suffering he witnessed amongst the smoking ruins.

Several times, Speer begged Hitler to visit Hamburg but each time Hitler refused. The King and Queen may have been pictured, picking their way amongst the rubble of London's East End; Churchill high on the back of an open car, two erect fingers held high in defiance; but Hitler would never be photographed consoling his people against a backdrop of a disintegrating Reich.

The bombing, on the face of it, appeared to be a battle between the bombers and the German defences. Essentially, it was a conflict between two men, Harris and Speer. Speer, still only in his mid-thirties, at the height of his intellectual powers, was a brilliant improviser with sufficient pragmatism to allow him to bend to events. Harris, in his early fifties, was a Trenchard; brave and charismatic but almost impossible to divert from what he saw as the true path. Harris hated all Germans; Speer admired the British in many ways. He envied them their industrial efficiency, their central overall control of their war effort. Contrary to general belief in German thoroughness, their industrial base was ill-organised, working at a mere fraction of its true potential. Hitler had expected a short war, a *Blitzkrieg,* with Britain backing out at the fall of France. His industry was not prepared for a long conflict and, in 1939, Britain was building far more aircraft than Germany. And there appeared to be no German to match de Havilland or Chadwick. Von Ohain at BMW, his He 178 rejected, had turned to developing the gas turbine engine but no one in Germany appeared to be taking him seriously. Even in mid-1942, nine-tenths of German industry was working a one shift system and consumer goods like refrigerators and radios were still in full production. Though they thought nothing of working slave labourers to death, it was still considered unseemly for German women to be recruited into industry.

With this enormous slack in the German industrial base, it was quite understandable that Speer's emotions had been affected, not by industrial damage, but by human suffering. In industrial terms, Harris could bomb and burn the city centres to his heart's content. Most industrial plant was located beyond the suburbs. Industry was doing very nicely. Taking the industrial capacity in January 1942 as a basic index of 100, by July 1942, despite all of Bomber Command's efforts, it had risen to 153. By July 1943 it was 229. Any industrial capacity lost as an incidental to the terror raid was replaced twice over within weeks. The defence implications of the unpredictable nature of Harris's targets was not Speer's concern. He had but one fear; that Harris would finally accept the futility of his campaign and turn to tactical bombing of resources vital to the German war machine. He had even drawn up a list; ball bearings; oil production; synthetic rubber; chemicals; communications.

He had reason to be concerned as, with escalating losses, there began a rising tide of disillusionment in Britain. Beaverbrook complained that "the achievements of our powerful and growing bomber force have been in no way commensurate with its potentialities, with the man-hours and materials expended on its expansion, nor with the losses it has sustained." Even Portal was wavering. He had returned from the Casablanca Conference in January 1943 with Roosevelt and Churchill's "Pointblank" directive ringing in his ears. "Your primary aim will be the progressive destruction and dislocation of the German military, industrial and economic system, and the undermining of the morale of the German people to the point where their capacity for armed resistance is fatally weakened." But Portal was now convinced the morale of the German people could not be so fatally weakened but appears to have lacked the strength to state this publicly. While seeming incapable of giving his subordinate direct orders, at least he could now inform Harris that, when the invasion came, Churchill had pledged all Bomber Command's efforts to support it and that Harris would have to take orders direct from the American Supreme Commander.

So Speer need not have feared. For Harris, time was running out if he was going to win the war all by himself. Nothing must now divert him. The clearest demonstration of Harris's attitude to what he disdainfully called panacea targets, was the part he did not play in the Schweinfurt raids. Ball bearings were top of Speer's list of economically vulnerable targets and Schweinfurt turned out 90 per cent of the German war machine's needs. Ball bearings also figured high on the priority list of Britain's Ministry of Economic Warfare. Air Commodore Bufton, Director of Bombing on the Air Staff, an outspoken advocate of the MEW and desperate that Harris should bomb Schweinfurt, was actively discouraged by Harris from visiting squadrons for fear his heretical views might take root. Baulked at Bomber Command HQ, Portal, Slessor, his assistant Chief of Staff, and Bufton, turned to the Americans.

Carl "Tooey" Spaatz was Commander of the American 8th Air

Force in Britain and was still in the throes of a murderously steep learning curve, such was the belief in the B17 and its Norden bomb sight. "Into a pickle barrel from 30,000 feet" had been the claim. Reality proved very different as the British had already learned. The early Boeing had undergone many major modifications by 1943. It flew at 325 mph at 25,000 feet with a ceiling of 37,000 feet, but, for all its 11 man crew, its bomb load never exceeded that of the Mosquito, 4,000 lbs, and it was a source of amusement to many a Mosquito pilot to fly rings round a B17 on one engine. When the RAF had considered acquiring a number, Saundby had listed amongst their defects that "the bomb load was uneconomical in relation to the crew and technical maintenance required." Flying in so-called combat boxes in unescorted daylight raids deep into Germany, they paid a heavy price for the industrial damage they caused. Losses were frequently over 10 per cent; 60 out of 376 one day, 60 out of 291 another.

But General Ira Eaker, the bomber commander, was allowed no respite. Eaker might have been junior to both Arnold and Spaatz but all three had been close friends since their days together at Rockwell Field back in 1918. An accomplished flyer - he had been personal pilot to General Douglas MacArthur - Eaker was also an intelligent man of letters with a graduate degree in journalism and cursed with the sensitivity to feel the loss of so many young crewmen. But friendship and sensitivity counted for naught as Arnold and Spaatz pressurised him to prove the capabilities of the B17 and the feasibility of their whole bombing strategy. Committed to daylight strategic bombing, they had no wish for a humiliating climb down to Harris's form of night bombing. Prompted by Portal and Bufton, they ordered Eaker to bomb Schweinfurt. On August 17, 1943, he did so and, combined with another raid on Regensburg, in one day lost 147 planes, some surviving but damaged beyond repair. In return for such grievous loss, a third of ball bearing production was destroyed and Speer's worst nightmare was being realised. Repeated attacks on this scale, he accepted, would bring Germany down. Bufton, equally convinced, pleaded with Harris to back Eaker up with a heavy night raid. But Harris, as if to show his disdain for the Americans, chose that night to lose 24 Lancasters, many with senior officers aboard, over the rocket bases at Peenemunde.

Though full production had resumed by late September, Speer made desperate efforts to disperse production from Schweinfurt and to acquire the entire output of neutral Sweden. Ball bearings were already being delivered direct from Schweinfurt to assembly plants with no stockpiling and Dr Philip Kessler, appointed as a special commissioner, was studying the use of porcelain ball bearings for non-precision machinery. Meanwhile, Eaker was being pressed hard by Arnold to repeat the raid. But such losses as they were suffering daily made regrouping almost impossible. In the week before the second raid two months later on October 14, the "Bloody One Hundredth" Group had lost 20 planes, eight out of 15 over Bremen, 12 out of 13 over Münster. During that two months, as the weeks went by, Speer began to wonder whether the enemy had really been so stupid as to have made it a "one-off" raid. But his instinct told him they would be back and he had taken the precaution of ringing the target with 300 88mm guns.

Out of the 291 planes that could be mustered for the second attack, 60 were lost. Though they did not know it, this time, due principally to the use of incendiaries, two-thirds of production was destroyed. The price the Americans paid was extreme but, with Harris's help, total success must have been within their grasp.

Harris however remained stubborn, declaring that dispersion must by now have been completed and quoting the inconclusive results of the other recent high profile strategic raid on the Dams. Not blessed with the ability of a Trenchard or a Harris to close the mind to the human cost, Eaker decided he could not possibly justify the losses by "going it alone" a third time, only to find his friends replace him with James "Jimmy" Doolittle.

And Speer breathed again.

Such unbearable losses over Schweinfurt heralded the end of the long distance unescorted daylight raids by the B17s. From then on, any raid beyond fighter escort range was strictly limited, sharply defined. The coming of the Mustang long-range fighter would change all that but, for the time being, the US 8th Air Force licked its wounds.

The Americans might have no compunction about removing their bomber commander but Harris appeared immune. Such was his popularity, both with his crews and with the population at large, that the effect of his sacking on morale was considered too great to contemplate. Independent to the last, he was determined to embark on the Battle of Berlin. Now made aware that, come the invasion, Bomber Command would be effectively taken from his hands, he would bank everything on his final fling at winning the war without Britain being committed to a major land battle. Though obliged to look on the Mosquito more favourably, his heavy bombers, in particular his Lancasters, would at last prove him correct. Cherwell's statistics had confirmed that they had destroyed 74 per cent of Hamburg. Now they would do to Berlin what they had done to Hamburg, only more so, and no nation's capital city on earth could withstand that. About that time, Churchill demonstrated a deeply felt moral conflict when, as recorded in the diary of one of his War Cabinet, Richard Casey, he became acutely disturbed on viewing aerial photographs of the devastation caused by Harris's tactics. "Are we beasts?" he cried out. "Are we taking this too far?" The prospect of Berlin in ruins however overcame his uncomfortable ambivalence and he gave the campaign his tacit support. At least it would placate the Russians in their constant demand for a second front.

It was at this stage that the Air Staff were presented with a paper prepared by Freeman's staff at the Ministry of Aircraft Production. Now that the Mosquito was capable of carrying a bomb load of 4,000 lbs to Berlin, something the B17s never achieved, and the average Lancaster bomb load over that distance was 8,000 lbs, figures for bombs dropped, targets hit, aircraft lost, aircrew trained, costs of resources and man-hours spent on construction and maintenance were correlated. The answer was brutally plain to see. For the same investment in industrial effort, the Mosquito would drop four-and-a-half times the weight of bombs as the Lancaster. The Lancaster took nearly three times the man-hours required to build a Mosquito and, on average, with its seven man crew, survived 28 night sorties before being written off. The average for the Mosquito with its two man crew was 92. Mosquito bomber losses on night sorties never exceeded one per cent, these occurring mostly amongst those carrying the Oboe navigational system which required the aircraft to fly over the target at constant speed, height and course. It was not unknown for a Mosquito to survive more than 200 sorties. Capable of flying to Berlin and back in under four hours, in mid-winter, with a fresh replacement crew, an individual Mosquito could raid the German capital twice in one night.

Even Harris could not utterly ignore such figures. Anxious that nothing should interfere with his heart's desire, the destruction of Berlin, at least he no longer actively impeded the Mosquitos as, at last, they set about the task at which they were supreme, pin-point daylight attacks. They joined the B17s in Operation Noball in their bombing of the V1 launching sites. The statisticians, now only too keen to extol the virtues of the Mosquito, especially at the expense of the Americans, proclaimed that the Mosquito, with 39.8 tons of bombs per site destroyed, far outscored the B17 on 191.1 tons. Over the coast at low level, climb to 3,000 feet, dive without warning to drop four 500 lb bombs, aimed and released by the pilot, and they were gone. Roy Ralston, one of the most distinguished of Mosquito pilots, seeing a train entering a tunnel, trapped it by closing the tunnel at both ends but the ultimate demonstration of the degree of accuracy now achieved was seen in the bombing of Amiens jail. In Operation Jericho, the walls of the prison were breached to allow French Resistance fighters, condemned to death, to make their escape.

Harris, a law unto himself, permitted by a Chief of Staff who stood in awe of him virtually to dictate his own bombing strategy, now turned his attention to the ultimate prize, Berlin. On November 18, 1943, the attack began. Losses mounted as the defences were strengthened. On the fifth raid at the beginning of December, 266 aircrew were lost, effectively the complement of two squadrons. On December 16, Oberleutnant Heinz Wolfgang Schnauffer shot down four Lancasters in the course of 12 minutes as they lumbered towards Berlin in a steady, predictable stream. In midwinter, conditions on board were appalling with frostbite not uncommon. Dulled wits due to exhaustion led to mistakes and collisions on landing. As the weeks went by, morale amongst the crew sagged. Stirlings and Halifaxes were withdrawn early in the raids, proving totally inadequate. Pathfinders, shepherding the main stream bombers began to report seeing some of the remaining Lancasters dropping their heavy bombs over the North Sea in search of those most cherished assets, height and speed. Though the carrying capacity of the Lancaster was now 12,000 lbs, the most they could carry to Berlin was 8,000 lbs. With a significant part of that jettisoned, little would be left for the target. It was a practice that became so prevalent that flash cameras were installed to photograph what lay below as the bombs were released.

While all this was going on, Mosquitos, flying to Berlin in varying modes; bombing, target marking, reconnoitring or simply intruding into night fighter airfields; completed 2,034 missions with the loss of 10 aircraft.

The inexorable Lancaster losses, up to 11 per cent at times, so damaging to morale, at least stiffened the backs of the spineless. The MEW continued to nag Portal over the importance of Schweinfurt. Air Marshall Bottomly urged Portal "... to destroy Schweinfurt at the earliest possible date." Both the British and American Air Staffs were now all in favour of "... attacking selected key industries known to be vulnerable and vital to the enemy's war effort." Still Harris objected. Writing to Bottomly, he complained that a major attack on Schweinfurt would not be "... a reasonable operation of war." And the reasoning behind his opinion? It was not the industrial effect produced - he dismissed this as requiring no more than six or seven raids to destroy completely - but that a town of 60,000 inhabitants did not warrant such attention.

There is no more fervent disciple than someone converted late to the faith and Portal was now fully convinced that area bombing was totally ineffective. With the backing of the combined Air Staffs, he ordered Harris to begin a campaign against Schweinfurt in conjunction with the Americans who would bomb by day. The combined attack began in February 1944 but it was too late. Speer had already dispersed production to Steyr, Erkner and Cannstatt as well as building up stockpiles from so-called neutral countries so that, despite production being reduced to 29 per cent by the time the attacks, again prematurely, were called off, no German machine ever suffered from the lack of a ball bearing.

Meanwhile, four more raids on Berlin cost 112 planes and 784 crew. The Pathfinder squadrons were being decimated. With overall losses amounting to 150 per cent of their November 1943 strength, they were obliged to recruit crews from the main force with no more than 10 sorties behind them. There was such concern over the heavy losses amongst the main force Lancasters that a special unit, The Lancaster Finishing School, was set up at Syerston in an attempt to improve aircrew skills. But the beginning of the end was signalled by a raid, not on Berlin itself, but on neighbouring Leipzig. Timing in Harris's raids was of the essence, concentrating the attacks in an attempt to overwhelm the defences. On this occasion, a strong tail wind caused chaos over the target with collisions galore. Out of 832 planes, 78 were lost. No air force could sustain such losses. There was one last raid on Berlin on March 24 when another 46 Lancasters were lost but Harris's dream was over. In the Battle of Berlin 2,690 bomber crewmen had died with another 987 taken prisoner. Over 1,000 aircraft were missing. It had been possible to look on the Battle of Hamburg as some sort of victory but, to most historians, the Battle of Berlin was a British defeat. But, like any cornered animal, it was at this point that Harris was at his most dangerous. Finally, driven into a corner, Harris showed his teeth, revealing the true nature of his bombing campaigns, stripped of any last vestige of hypocritical justification.

On March 30, 1944, with all the petulance of a child's destruction of a toy that fails to satisfy, he sent his heavy bombers to Nuremberg. Why Nuremberg? It was deep in enemy territory, impossible to reach without flying over heavily defended routes. It was of no industrial importance, considered by the Allied Chiefs of Staff as of no strategic significance. It was best known for being the birthplace of Nazism. Having failed over Berlin, was Harris intent on destroying the Nazi shrine? Mosquitos which reconnoitred the city in daylight returned to report thick, total cloud cover and the meteorological report was equally unfavourable. No one, including Saundby, dreamed that Harris would do anything but postpone the raid. But the order was given.

A measure of how slowly the heavily laden bombers flew and in such a steady, predictable stream, was the night's tally of just one night fighter pilot. Oberleutnant Martin Becker shot down three Lancasters and three Halifaxes. Landing to refuel and re-arm, he still had time to shoot down another Halifax. Out of the 569 planes involved, 95 were missing, 79 thought to have been shot down by night fighters. 545 crew died in one night, more than the total lost during the whole of the Battle of Britain and 101 were taken prisoner. Due to the thick cloud, the bombing area measured 10 by 15 miles, the small town of Lauf, 10 miles to the east of Nuremberg taking the brunt of the attack. Well over 100 of the main stream bombed Schweinfurt by mistake, 55 miles to the north east of Nuremberg. Little more than 500 tons of bombs fell on Nuremberg itself.

This, after four-and-a-half years of war, thousands of young lives sacrificed and vast resources poured into the heavy bombers at the expense of other branches of the services.

Surely, it could be tolerated no longer? If Portal lacked the moral fibre to grasp the nettle, surely Arthur Tedder, now Deputy Supreme Allied Commander under Eisenhower and with years of experience in tactical bombing in the Mediterranean, would have no such difficulty? Surely, Churchill must now come off the fence?

But no; Harris survived. So deeply had the Trenchard Touch penetrated the psyche, not only of the devoted aircrews but that of the man in the street, that, such would be the dire result on morale, both fighting and civilian, that Churchill dare not remove him. Anyway, the Second Front was looming and, under an ultimate American command, Harris could at last be kept on a tighter rein. The Mustang fighter, with its Rolls Royce Merlin engine, was arriving to compensate for the Fortress's inadequacies and night bombing of city centres would lose its spectator appeal in cinemas up and down the country in competition with the sight of rippling bomb bursts, clearly seen straddling factories and communication centres.

Let him stay. Let him see the war out to reap honours and have his statue unveiled by royalty. But the ultimate honour, a peerage, would be denied him, blocked by one of his own air-crew, Lord Stansgate.

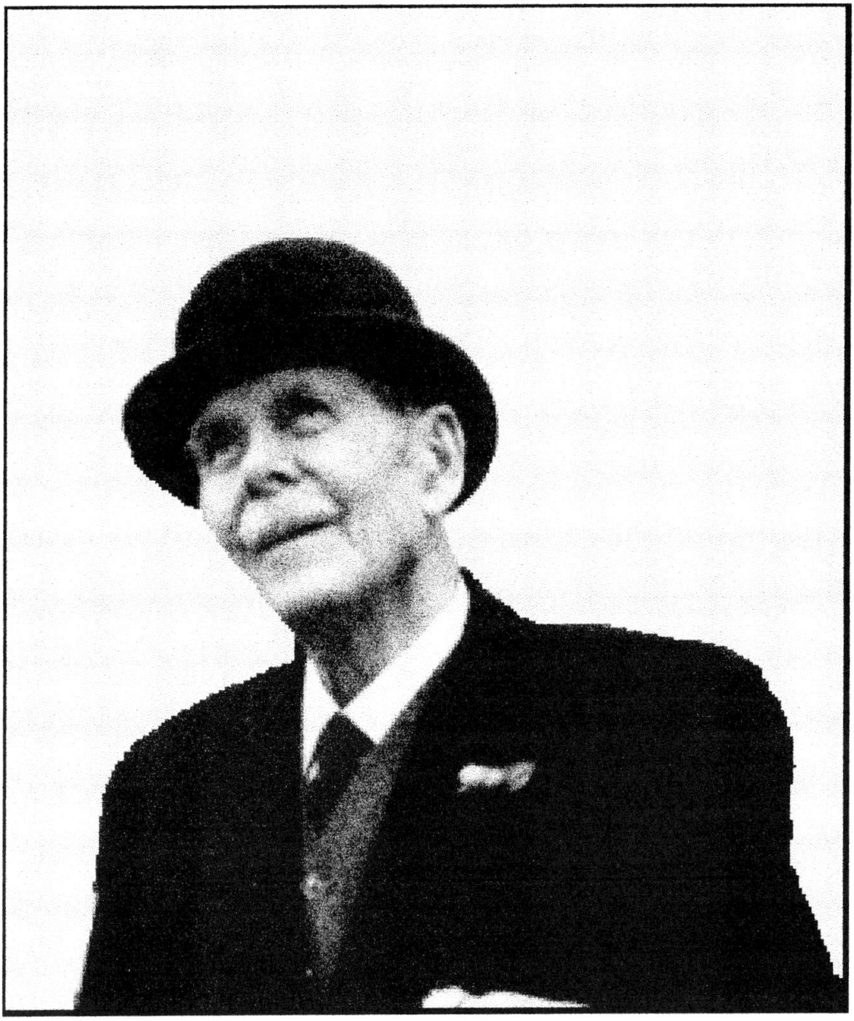

Chapter Twelve

It was over. With one grisly exception, a night of madness over Dresden, the 30 year myth of terror bombing was at an end. It had been shown to be what it was, a ghastly misconception engendered within the personalities of a few men, honest and true but misguided. It had resulted in thousands of the finest young men being sacrificed on the altar of a false god, not to mention the deaths of countless thousands of German men, women and children. Estimated figures in an immediately post-war survey would be given as 3,600,000 dwellings destroyed, 300,000 civilians killed, 780,000 wounded and 7,500,000 made homeless. And all to no avail. News of minor episodes of civil uprising would have been suppressed in any country at war, as indeed occurred in Britain, but such was the stoicism of the German people, stiffened further under the watchful eye of the Gestapo, there had been no major civil unrest, no rioting in the streets, no threat to the Nazi hierarchy. It is doubtful if Hitler lost one night's sleep over the whole affair. Certainly, this time, there were no grounds for the German army to accuse the civil population of stabbing it in the back.

One can only speculate as to Trenchard's thoughts at that time. He was still around, a spent force in military terms though not for want of trying. Shortly before his retirement from the RAF, as if to make sure everyone had got the message, he spelt out one last time, in a paper to the Imperial Defence College, what he saw as the primary task of the RAF.

"The object of all three services is the same; to defeat the enemy nation, not merely its Army, Navy or Air Force. It is not, however, necessary for an Air Force, in order to defeat the enemy nation, to defeat its armed forces first. ... There may be many who, realising that this new form of warfare will extend to the whole community the horrors and sufferings hitherto confined to the battlefield, would urge that the air offensive should be restricted to the zone of the opposing armed forces. If this restriction were feasible, I should be the last to quarrel with it, but it is not feasible."

Knowing the nature of the man, it was unreasonable to expect Trenchard to go into retirement passively. But what could he do? John Salmond, his successor, proved far too good a Chief of Air Staff to give grounds for interference - anyway, he would only have been preaching to the converted - and he had to be content with battling in ferocious debate against Beatty in the House of Lords over the command of the Fleet Air Arm. Ramsey MacDonald offered Trenchard the post of Commissioner of the Metropolitan Police. Sir John Anderson, the civil servant supreme, weighed in, cajoling Trenchard, stressing the need for reform to restore discipline and efficiency. There were hints of corruption. But Trenchard refused, saying he wanted only to be left in peace, free, no doubt, to snipe and criticise at Government policy. Then, in 1931, came the financial crisis and MacDonald's coalition government's 10 per cent pay cuts in the public services. There was a minor mutiny in the Navy up at Invergordon and mutterings of a possible police strike in London. Once more, MacDonald approached Trenchard to become Commissioner, hinting that it was the wish of the King that he took the post. This time he accepted. What else could an old soldier do when King and country called?

That Trenchard was a success as Commissioner of the Metropolitan Police is beyond doubt. Honest, utterly incorruptible, a gifted organiser and morale booster, he was admirably qualified for the job. One of the first tasks he set himself was the establishment of a police college to attract talented young men to the force. Overcoming the resistance of the Police Federation which, with its dedication to promotion through the ranks, had scuppered a previously proposed National Police College, Trenchard realised his dream when, in May 1934, the Police

College at Hendon was officially opened by the Prince of Wales. But it did not last, gradually running down until its closure in 1939. After the war, in 1946, the Labour Government revived a college designed to train those officers destined for high rank.

But Trenchard's mind still ran on military matters. The fact that he was now a public servant and thereby unable publicly to criticise government policy, did not preclude him from making his feelings known. There is a subtle difference between expressing an opinion and criticism.

In 1932 he submitted to the Air Staff a paper on the defence of Singapore which he saw as primarily an Air Force responsibility. But Baldwin, now Prime Minister, anxious to placate the Navy, opted for the fixed heavy naval guns. Trenchard was equally unsuccessful in his attempts to dissuade John Salmond, the last of his personally trained staff, from resigning in favour of his younger brother, a man dying of cancer who held the post for six months only before giving way to Ellington with whom Trenchard had no vestige of rapport. By 1934, Trenchard's frustration drove him to request his release from duties at Scotland Yard but the King, influenced by a Prime Minister only too anxious to keep a loose cannon tied down, persuaded Trenchard to stay another two years. But, in 1935, he walked out, destined never to be used in any purposeful capacity again.

He turned to politics for which he was far from being ideally equipped, trying all ways to depose Hankey, the Cabinet Secretary, with whom he had clashed most often over defence. He failed. He was unfortunate also in his friendship with Churchill. Of similar temperament, their mutual respect survived blistering arguments but it was at a time when Churchill languished in the political desert and any friend must necessarily remain there with him. Powerless, he had to come to terms with the Navy being granted control of the

The Trenchard Touch

Fleet Air Arm as Chamberlain logically devolved command of all landborne aircraft to the RAF, all seaborne planes to the Navy.

But it was not simply political frustration that forced Trenchard out into commerce. He was short of money and had sons to educate. His directorships of Goodyear and the United Africa Company resulted in his happy return to Nigeria. In 1937, in the course of his travels, he dined with Goering who began by showing him great respect and deference. When drunk, however, Goering left Trenchard in no doubt what lay in store for Britain.

When war started, Trenchard immediately offered his services but was rejected. It did not prevent him from visiting France, stirring old memories by urging the Advanced Striking Force to bomb cities in Germany at a time when such offensive action was forbidden for fear of reprisals. Then the Germans bombed the heart out of Rotterdam and his friend Churchill came to power, offering Trenchard the post of General Officer Commanding Home Forces in the event of invasion. But, again, they quarrelled bitterly as Churchill listened to the powers that Trenchard demanded to go with the position. Churchill had no intention of allowing anyone under him to possess such power. He would take orders from no one. He changed his mind, offering Trenchard the challenge of reorganising Military Intelligence. Again, with characteristic honesty, Trenchard talked himself out of a job, doubting his own ability to carry out such a task.

Churchill had done his best for his old friend. He could do no more as Trenchard became a rather pathetic figure, touring air bases, a mere shadow of his previous powerful self.

"The only good German is a dead one," a statement, like so much war time propaganda, simply not true. The campaign of area bombing was not alone in its failure, not unique in terms of bravery and human sacrifice. Driven by political or religious beliefs, military pride or simple patriotism, hundreds of German men and women gave their lives in heroic but futile attempts to rid their country of Hitler and all he stood for. Some acted in splendidly courageous isolation; others formed themselves into groups.

One such group, the Kreisau Circle led by Count Helmuth James von Moltke, was drawn largely from the military sons of old aristocratic German families. Their greatest problem was their refusal to contemplate assassination, even of someone as evil as Hitler, viewing it as cold-blooded murder. As a result, they spent most of their time in philosophical discussion without any appreciable effect. Another group, the White Rose, comprised mainly of Catholic students in Munich given to much youthful idealism but little action, were understandably discouraged when a localised student revolt came to nothing, resulting only in its leaders, Hans Scholl and his sister, Sophie, barely 20 years old, being beheaded. Yet another group, an unlikely brotherhood of extreme right and left wing activists, brought together by Beppo Romer, the former Oberland Freikorps leader, had been smashed by the Gestapo in 1942. A sizeable group, 150 of their members were tried before the Peoples Court and 45 executed.

Those involved in the September Plot of 1938, so shamefully abandoned by the British Foreign Office, were still around in 1943 but now fragmented, no longer of significance as a group but still individuals with a part to play. Gördeler, the erstwhile Mayor of Leipzig, continued to make contact with London via his friends in international banking but his demands for a unilateral peace in return for Hitler's death were repeatedly rejected out of hand. Oster at the Abwehr was also still active. It was forged papers, provided by him, that allowed religious leaders to visit Sweden where they were in contact with Dr George Bell, Bishop of Chichester, well known to them for his outspoken criticism of Britain's bombing campaign. But similar messages, carried by the Bishop to Anthony Eden at the British Foreign Office, including a list of all the conspirators on whom they could rely, were of no avail.

Another attempt on Hitler's life had come close to success. Operation Flash in March 1943 was launched without any apparent idea of what should follow. At the centre of the plot were two high ranking German officers, General von Tresckow, Chief of Staff at Field Marshal Kluge's Army Group Centre on the Russian Front, and General Friedrich Olbricht, Chief of the Army General Office and a devout Christian, with Fabian von Schlabrendorff, a junior on Olbricht's staff, more than willing to play the active, physical role. Hitler planned to travel from the Wolfsschauze at Rastenburg to the Army HQ behind Smolensk, a journey requiring transport by air. A bomb would be placed on the plane on the return flight. Their fellow conspirators at the Abwehr, Canaris and Oster, knew of the attempt and provided the bombs; British bombs. These bombs, captured from those dropped by the RAF to the French Resistance, had one advantage over their German counterparts - they did not hiss when armed. They also had a proven track record, having been successfully used in the assassination of Heydrich.

On March 13, 1943, Hitler arrived in Smolensk. At dinner, one of Hitler's staff readily agreed to carry back to Berlin a parcel, comprised, he was informed, of two bottles of brandy, a gift for a friend of Schlabrendorff's. Schlabrendorff delivered the package to the plane, pressing a button to smash a small bottle of a corrosive acid which, in time, would eat through a wire, thus releasing a trigger mechanism on to the detonator. But Hitler landed safely. The detonator had failed to explode as Schlabrendorff found out when he courageously retrieved the package from Rastenburg, finding his way into the heart of the Wolf's Lair to replace it with genuine bottles of brandy.

In all, it was a diffuse, thinly spread resistance, brave but amateur in nature, which cried out for an inspirational leader, someone of impeccable background, of proven courage and, above all, with access to Hitler. Fate decreed that the cry should be answered as Tresckow and Schlabrendorff were joined at Army Group Centre HQ by Claus von Stauffenberg.

His impeccable background? A great grandson of Gneisenau, the founder of the Prussian General Staff, Lieutenant Colonel Klaus Phillip Schenk, Count von Stauffenberg's father had been Privy Chamberlain to the last King of Württenberg. His mother was Countess von Uxkull-Gyllenbrand. Catholic by religion, monarchist by tradition, congenial and cultivated by breeding, Stauffenberg had gone to war as his duty to his country. His bravery? He had fought through Poland and France with the 6th Panzer Division. In Russia the brutality of the SS had sickened him and he had managed to transfer to North Africa under Rommel where he had been wounded, losing an eye, one hand and two fingers from the remaining hand. It was while convalescing that he had determined to rid Germany of Hitler.

By September 1943, he was back in Berlin on General Olbricht's Staff at the Army General Office, teaching himself with three fingers on his left hand, to arm British bombs, using a pair of tongs. Finally proficient, on Boxing Day, deputising for his chief, he joined the noon conference at Rastenberg, a bomb in his briefcase, only to find that Hitler had decided to spend Christmas at Obersalzburg.

The defining moment was his meeting with Tresckow. Only then did he realise the extent of the resistance movement, that even his own chief, Olbricht, was committed. He was a brilliant young staff officer. He now turned those talents to good effect. Though junior in rank to many involved, he virtually took command, revitalising with his charm and enthusiasm the older jaded conspirators.

First, he argued, there was little point in killing Hitler if there was no plan to deal, within minutes, hours and days of Hitler's death, with the remaining Nazi leaders, the Gestapo and the SS. It was readily agreed that in the new government, Beck would be the Head of State, Goerdeler the Chancellor and Field Marshal von Witzleban Commander in Chief of the Wehrmacht. But how, militarily, was this to be achieved? It was at this point that the simple soldiers found in Stauffenberg the lateral thinker the whole movement had lacked until then.

The Valkyrie were, according to Norse mythology, beautiful maidens, servants of the god Odin, who hovered over the battle field, choosing from the slain those worthy of being admitted to Valhalla. The Nazi leaders, no one more so than Albert Speer, were fully aware of the consequences should a mass revolt occur amongst the vast numbers of forced labourers in their country. The Valkyrie plan had been drawn up in preparation for such a crisis and had resulted in the formation of the Home Army under the command of General Fritz Fromm, himself a wavering conspirator. To counter any serious threat to the Third Reich from within its own borders, a command structure existed to ensure immediate control of Berlin, Vienna, Munich and Cologne. This, turned round to the conspirators advantage, could prove the ideal cover for their preparations and would be extended, within hours of Hitler's death, to the Home Army's occupation of the national broadcasting service, Berlin's two radio stations, telephone and telegraph services, together with the Reich Chancellery, the Ministries and the Gestapo HQ. General Fellgiebel, Chief of Signals on Hitler's HQ

Staff, had promised to render all Nazi operational centres incommunicado. All that would be required would be an order from Fromm.

On Olbricht's recommendation, promoted to full Colonel, Stauffenberg became Fromm's Chief of Staff of the Home Army, perfectly placed: one, to keep the faltering Fromm on track; two, to replace him with General Höpner, the brilliant tank commander, cashiered by Hitler and forbidden even to wear uniform, should Fromm's nerve fail him at the crucial moment.

Detailed planning went on throughout the later months of 1943 and into 1944 as a sense of urgency began to permeate the group. The Gestapo was closing in on the Abwehr and Oster had already been dismissed and placed under house arrest. Several Abwehr agents abroad had defected to the British, taking code books with them. Hitler, furious, ordered Himmler to take over from Canaris. Soon after, von Moltke was arrested and the Kreisau Circle smashed. A Russian offensive was expected at any time. Invasion by the Western Allies was imminent. The war in Italy was going badly. They must hurry if they were to save Germany from total destruction and humiliation. But what was finally required was some national icon, someone of international repute, respected and trusted by the Western Allies, to publicly throw his weight behind the coup when the time came. Someone like a serving Field Marshal. Von Runstedt was approached but, while assuring them of confidentiality, refused to go back on his oath to Hitler. Von Manstein, ever the opportunist, weighed the odds and declined the offer.

But, unknown to Stauffenberg, just such a man was being welcomed into the fold in France. The Desert Fox, Field Marshal Erwin Rommel, had always been considered a Nazi but, on being appointed to command Army Group B in the west, he had come under the influence of two old friends, General Alexander von Falkenhausen, the Military Governor of Belgium, and General Karl-Heinrich von Stulpnagel, Military Governor of France, both committed conspirators. Also to sway Rommel was another old friend, Dr Karl Stroelin, the Oberbürgermeister of Stuttgart who was witnessing, day by day, his beloved city being reduced to rubble by allied bombing. Finally converted, Rommel declared to Stroelin, "I believe it is my duty to come to the rescue of Germany."

And, of course, there was still Eddie Chapman. Himmler may have taken command of Military Intelligence at OKW but a hard core of the old Abwehr staff still remained and Eddie was still in touch with both them and MI5. His mission to America had been cancelled and he had spent all his money on a protracted holiday in Norway. On his return, he had been awarded the Iron Cross and had been briefed widely on security operations, including those relating to the Führer's personal safety. Ideally placed to act as a link between the conspirators and British Intelligence while, no doubt, not averse to miss the fighting to come, his constant requests to be dropped back in Britain the Nazis had taken as evidence of his commitment to the cause.

On the night of June 21, 1944, as the Russians were crushing the German Army Group Centre on their way to Poland, Eddie Chapman was granted his wish. Dropped from the sky once more, he landed on this occasion at Six Mile Bottom in Cambridgeshire. With £6,000 in his pocket, he reported to the nearest police station where the duty officer told him, "Don't be silly. Go to bed."

"That's exactly what they said last time," Eddie complained, only too anxious to relay to his British masters the details of the Stauffenberg plan.

Once again Chapman, the great survivor, would escape

retribution, safely tucked away in Britain as, on July 20, 1944, the botched assassination attempt by Stauffenberg and Hitler's miraculous survival resulted in the decimation of the conspirators. Stauffenberg and Olbricht were executed in the army courtyard on Bendlerstrasse the same night. Of the 154 brave men known to have died as a result of their failure, a few cheated the executioner by taking their own lives. They were the lucky ones. Many of the remainder died in the most gruesome circumstances, recorded on film for Hitler's pleasure. Many good Germans were dead ones, some no doubt helped on their way by the list of those most likely to have been involved, published by Duff Cooper's Ministry. And Eddie Chapman? What became of him? He survived to a venerable old age, finding himself once more back in a British court, charged under the Official Secrets Act as his escapades were immortalised in book and film.

The disastrous raid on Nuremberg had taken place on the night of March 30, 1944. On April 15, Harris and Bomber Command were delivered into the firm grip of General Dwight D. Eisenhower. There would be no more area bombing. Fifteen months before, in January 1943, at the watershed conference at Casablanca, Portal, one of Trenchard's protégés, had finally become convinced that bombing alone could not win the war and had agreed that, when the time came, the RAF's Bomber Command would put its entire effort towards the preparation for the invasion of Europe. He now set about honouring that pledge. For the first time, both British and American air forces would work in harmony towards a common goal.

To ensure this a new personality appeared on the European scene, that of Arthur Tedder. Here was a man whose middle name might have been co-operation and his appointment as Eisenhower's Deputy Supreme Commander, in overall command of all Allied Air Forces in Europe, was the result of the part he had played in the North Africa victories, triumphs due in great measure to his close co-operation with a man, notoriously difficult to get on with, Bernard Law Montgomery. Tedder and Portal were of comparable rank but if there were to be a power struggle between the Deputy Supreme Commander and the Chief of Air Staff, there was going to be but one victor. Portal, in his early days as Chief of Air Staff, had fought off the challenge of the Army who saw the Air Force as primarily an Army support unit, in true Trenchard tradition stubbornly maintaining the RAF's independence with its right to choose its own targets, the centres of civil population. It had only been in keeping then that he had chosen Harris as his C in C Bomber Command, knowing him to be a latterday Trenchard, only to find as time went by and Portal's own dedication to area bombing had begun to waver, that he had appointed a rigid thinker, impossible to influence let alone command. But now there was a new man at the top, someone who had just concluded a brilliantly successful campaign, someone who was unlikely to feel inhibited, dealing with a subordinate responsible for what was now largely seen as a costly failure. From now on Harris would do as he was told. Bomber Command would co-operate fully with the American 8th Air Force with but one aim in mind, easing the task of their brothers in arms destined to land on the beaches.

Apart from tying down German defence manpower, desperately needed elsewhere, and pacifying Russian demands for more action by the Western Allies, the RAF campaign had achieved little but, up till then, the US 8th Air Force had not exactly covered itself in glory either. They too had made the fundamental mistake of choosing the wrong aircraft, thereby committing themselves to a method of bombing that had come close to disaster. They too in peacetime had preached the doctrine that the bomber, particularly the heavily armed types, unescorted in daylight, would always get through. Stacked in what were confidently predicted to be impregnable "combat boxes", the brainchild of Colonel Curtis E. LeMay, nothing could possibly stand in their way as they bombed with pin-point accuracy using the much lauded Norden sight. But there had been one inconsistency in their theory of pin-point bombing to which they had developed a facultative blindness. It would be impossible to reconcile pin-point accuracy with flying in formation. True pin-point bombing would only be possible if they would be prepared to break formation over the target, queue up in line and bomb individually with all the vulnerability such predictable tactics must inevitably bring with it. In reality it was found that simultaneous bombing by a combat box, timed predominantly on the aim of the lead bomber, resulted in only 20 per cent of bombs falling within a 1000 feet radius of the target.

With consummate bravery, the Americans had pressed their attacks against withering odds until the raids on Schweinfurt in October 1943. After the grievous losses there, all unescorted raids deep into enemy territory had been suspended. It had taken them 15 months to learn the lesson the crews of the Blenheims and Wellingtons had so painfully absorbed in a matter of weeks in 1939.

But all that was about to change. The heavy bomber was to be saved by the P51 Mustang, a fighter with a Rolls Royce engine, built in America to RAF specifications, the first plane for more than two years to match the Mosquito for speed and range. American bomber losses in October 1943 were 9.1 per cent; in February 1944, after the arrival of the Mustang, 3.5 per cent. Under their protection, strategic bombing in daylight at last became a feasible proposition as they set about a systematic attack on German airframe factories.

It must be said that this campaign too, overall, was a failure. The first truly co-ordinated campaign of strategic bombing fell short of its objective due, not to any lack of bravery, commitment or planning but to the resilient nature of the target chosen. The bombing had an immediate effect - deliveries of Me109 fighters dropped from 725 in July 1943 to 536 in September - but it was transient. Germany had gone into the war with a vast excess in industrial capacity. They had not foreseen such a great demand for fighter aircraft but, after the first major raids, the control of aircraft production, now a matter of the greatest urgency, passed from the Luftwaffe to Speer. As a result, despite every known airframe factory being hit in February 1944, 39,000 aircraft were delivered in 1944 as compared with 15,000 in 1942. Production not only recovered after the heaviest of raids but increased and, reluctantly bowing to the inevitable, the attacks were eventually called off.

And yet, it was claimed later by the Germans that they had no more than 80 operational planes with which to oppose the landings on D-day. The likeliest cause for this was not a dearth of airframes so much as the lack of trained combat pilots to put in them. The German fighters that had mauled the early American unescorted daylight raids had not got away unscathed. Many a bomber, fatally wounded, had taken its destroyer with it. But the Mustang had proved such an outstanding success in protecting the bomber formations that they were soon given orders not merely to protect but to seek out and destroy enemy fighters in offensive sweeps ahead and around. Giulio Douhet, the true prophet, was at last to be proved correct; for strategic bombing to be successful, the opposing air defence must first be rendered impotent. Such was the Mustang's superiority over German fighters which had progressed little from those that had taken part in the Battle of Britain, that, to many an American pilot, it was like "shooting ducks in a barrel" as they took their toll amongst the veteran German pilots. The Germans might be adept and resourceful at airframe manufacture but producing a trained, experienced combat pilot took time.

Switching the attack to the synthetic oil refineries was much more rewarding. In August 1943, a daylight, low level attack on Ploesti in Rumania had proved costly and tentative raids on plant in the Ruhr had been carried out in September. But it was not until May 1944, with the invasion safely under way, that a maximum sustained effort could be launched. Thirteen plants were identified as producing the bulk of high grade oils, particularly aviation fuel, and, of these, Leuna in Eastern Germany was the largest. Many aircrews would have good cause to rue the long and dangerous flight to the Saale River valley but what happened at Leuna was typical of the campaign as a whole. Time and again Leuna was put out of action only to recover 75 per cent production in a matter of weeks. But the attacks were sustained, the effect cumulative and in June Speer was reporting losses of aviation fuel of up to 90 per cent. With singleness of purpose - there were no other more demanding distractions now - and with a steadily deteriorating German air defence, overall production was bound to suffer, however skilful Speer had become at manipulating his slave labourers. Though the oil production was still 15 per cent normal capacity at the war's end, overall production during the months of attack between May and December 1944, was down to nine per cent, a level inevitably to have significant consequences such as the capture intact by the Russians of over a thousand tanks, immobilised for want of fuel, on the Vistula. Of more significance to the B17s and the Liberators were the severe restrictions imposed on the duration of training flights for tyro German fighter pilots, so desperate to get to grips with the bombers. Once more, nothing was succeeding quite like success.

Harris was not slow to cash in on that success. "The triumph of the offensive against oil," he wrote after the war, "was complete and indisputable," adding, patronisingly, "Here was a panacea target which offered the greatest advantage with no considerable effort," going on to claim that the campaign could not have been a success without the co-operation of the RAF. This from the man who had refused to come to the aid of the Americans over Schweinfurt.

And, while all this was going on, what of the Mosquitos? Was use being made of their great potential, so studiously overlooked by Harris in his rush for mass destruction?

As a reconnaissance aircraft it had reigned supreme. With its range, speed and ceiling it had been almost inviolate. The Americans had acknowledged this, at least one complete reconnaissance squadron being converted to Mosquitos, one of which had just lowered the west to east trans-Atlantic record to five hours forty minutes. They had proved the favourite aircraft amongst the night fighter aces in preference to planes designed specifically for that purpose. And, of course, the Pathfinders had abandoned their Lancasters for the Mosquito; Group Captain Leonard Cheshire, the prince of Pathfinders, had won his VC in one. In February 1944, reminiscent of their previous low level attacks on Gestapo Headquarters, they had carried out a truly pin-point bombing raid on the jail at Amiens, breaching the wall to allow 250 resistance fighters to escape and, after June, their success rate at knocking out V1 rocket sites was unsurpassed. But this was using the Mosquito as virtually a ground attack aircraft. Were they ever to be given a chance to prove themselves as de Havilland had visualised; as fast, unarmed, unescorted bombers?

In April 1944, Sir Edgar Ludlow-Hewitt wrote to the Vice

Chief of Air Staff. This was the man who had "blown the whistle" on Trenchard's bombing philosophy in 1939 and had paid for it by spending the war, side-tracked into the sinecure post of Inspector General of the RAF. "As the enemy's night defences improve," he wrote, "the value of the very fast night bomber which can carry an effective load becomes more and more apparent." He could only have had the Mosquito in mind and when this led, at last, to the formation of the Light Night Striking Force, de Havilland's bomber finally, tardily, came into its own. Composed entirely of Mosquitos with their own Pathfinders using H2S navigation, they roamed the skies almost unmolested. Capable of carrying a 4,000 lb bomb load to Berlin, something beyond the capabilities of the B17, sometimes twice in one night, they were delivering twice the load of the Lancaster when compared in terms of crew man-hours. The apogee of the Force's operations came in the spring of 1945 when 100 Mosquitos bombed Berlin on 36 consecutive nights, in so doing producing, ironically, an effect for which Harris and his heavies had striven so long and so hard but failed to achieve. Dr Goebbels, in his capacity as Mayor of Berlin, fearing for the first time civil unrest, expressed genuine alarm such constant bombardment was having on civilian morale.

In July 1945, Trenchard stood amid the devastation that was Berlin. What buildings had remained standing after relentless air attack had been razed to the ground by a rampant, vengeful Russian army. Dazed Germans, eyes downcast, stumbled like sleepwalkers amongst the rubble of what once had been a proud city. Deep, wide urban canyons, ramrod straight between brooding Teutonic monoliths, had been reduced to narrow tortuous pathways between piles of stone, brick and concrete. Black crosses, roughly painted on crumbling walls, were the only epitaphs to unclaimed corpses beneath.

It was all over; the fighting, the dying; the fear, the courage; the victories, the disasters, the cock-ups; the lethal misconceptions of honest men. What must have been going through the mind of the sad old belligerent as he saw at firsthand the effects of total air war on the heart of a city? Would his conscience have pricked him, even for a moment? Would any doubts, never to be admitted, have crept into his mind?

Or would he have been beyond cold analysis, still coming to terms, as he must have been, with the heart-breaking pride of losing three of his sons, two soldiers and an airman, in battle?

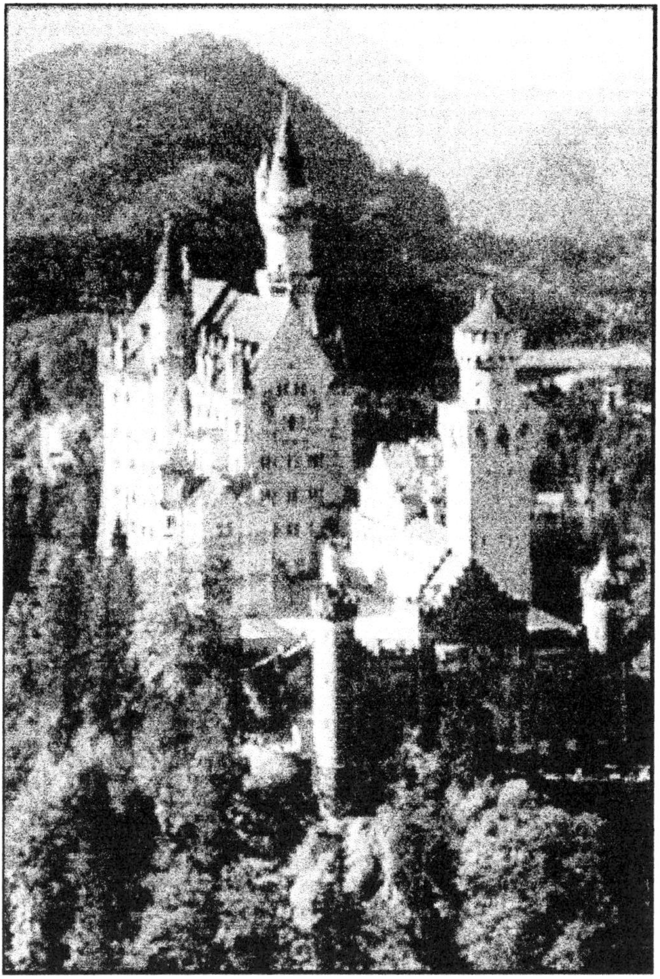

Epilogue

What might have been if only ...

On March 30, 1944, with all the petulance of a child's destruction of a toy that fails to satisfy, Harris sent his heavy bombers to Nuremberg. Why Nuremberg? It was deep in enemy territory, impossible to reach without flying over heavily defended routes. It was of no industrial importance, considered by the Allied Chiefs of Staff as of no strategic significance. It was best known for being the birthplace of Nazism. Having failed over Berlin, was Harris intent on destroying the Nazi shrine? Mosquitos which reconnoitred the city in daylight returned to report thick, total cloud cover and the meteorological report was equally unfavourable. No one, including Saundby, dreamed that Harris would do anything but postpone the raid. But the order was given.

A measure of how slowly the heavily laden bombers flew and in such a steady, predictable stream, was the night's tally of just one night fighter pilot. Oberleutnant Martin Becker shot down three Lancasters and three Halifaxes. Landing to refuel and re-arm, he still had time to shoot down another Halifax. Out of the 569 planes involved, 95 were missing, 79 thought to have been shot down by night fighters. 545 crew died in one night, more than the total lost during the whole of the Battle of Britain and 101 were taken prisoner. Due to the thick cloud, the bombing area measured 10 by 15 miles, the small town of Lauf, 10 miles to the east of Nuremberg taking the brunt of the attack. Well over 100 of the main stream bombed Schweinfurt by mistake, 55 miles to the north east of Nuremberg. Little more than 500 tons of bombs fell on Nuremberg itself.

This, after four-and-a-half years of war, thousands of young lives sacrificed and vast resources poured into the heavy bombers at the expense of other branches of the services.

The Trenchard Touch

Surely, it could be tolerated no longer? If Portal lacked the moral fibre to grasp the nettle, surely Arthur Tedder, now Deputy Supreme Allied Commander under Eisenhower and with years of experience in tactical bombing in the Mediterranean, would have no such difficulty? Surely, Churchill must now come off the fence?

Ultimately, it was left to Churchill to make the decision that inevitably would have an impact on the country's morale. He alone carried sufficient authority to soften the blow to a nation's pride as Arthur Harris, a national icon, was sacked to be replaced by a man of vision and intelligence, Edgar Ludlow-Hewitt. Surely now, things must be different. Changes in strategic planning must inevitably follow the replacement of a rigid, tunnel visioned personality with someone capable of lateral thinking, a man convinced since the debacles of 1939 that the future of bombing lay in the fast, unarmed bomber. Within weeks of his appointment, the Light Night Striking Force of Mosquitos came into being while the main force Lancasters were soon pounding lines of communication alongside the American 8th Air Force in preparation for D-day. There were also plans to define a role for the Lancasters of which they were uniquely capable. They were to be modified to carry the 12,000 lb. Tallboy and 22,000 lb. Grand Slam bombs, loads no other plane in the world at that time could match.

But, as Eddie Chapman dropped from the night sky into the leafy lanes of Cambridgeshire's Six Mile Bottom, Ludlow-Hewitt's innovative powers were about to be challenged. Chapman had been on the end of Mosquito bombing attacks, was well aware of their characteristic almost silent approach. He was also privy to every detail of the Stauffenberg plan. Surely, he thought, three or four highly skilled professional pilots, each with 4,000 lbs. of explosive to throw away, were more likely to be successful than one brave but half blind, one handed amateur trying to change the course of history with a few pounds of explosive carried in a brief-case? Surely the accuracy that had been brought to several Gestapo HQs and the Amiens jail could be put to more fundamental purpose? The only problem, as far as Chapman could see, was that the target he had in mind was constantly on the move, rarely undefended.

Which was why he was in such a hurry to make contact with his controllers at MI5.

Hitler was at his Berghof on the Obersalzberg, high above Berchtesgaden. But MI5 already knew that. Bletchley Park had been monitoring communications between the Berghof and the Wolf's Lair at Rastenberg. They were well aware that Field Marshal von Kluge, scenting military disaster on his front, was anxious to spread the responsibility. Too often he had seen what happened to Army commanders when the Führer was looking for a scapegoat. And it was now common knowledge amongst the high command that Hitler, previously so infallible, was showing every sign of being rattled. Olbricht reported seeing him during conferences at the Berghof, either pushing charts around the table in a daze, his eyes unfocused, or ranting at his Generals for no good reason. Repeatedly, von Kluge was begging the Army's Commander in Chief to visit Rastenberg to see for himself the seriousness of the situation.

But did MI5 know, Chapman asked, that there was a plot for an Army Colonel, by the name of von Stauffenberg, to assassinate Hitler when he arrived in Rastenberg? Again, MI5 showed no surprise at the news. Did they realise, Chapman persisted, what little chance of success there would be, either at the Berghof or at Rastenberg with their perimeter fences, armed patrols, checkpoints, reinforced bunkers? That did not seem to concern MI5.

Ever since 1941, the professional killers of Section X, the German Section of the Special Operations Executive, had dreamed of assassinating Hitler. Their Operation Foxley had been minutely researched along the lines of a sniper attack during Hitler's routine morning walk from the Berghof to the Teehaus on the Mooslaner Kopf, only to be discarded ultimately as impracticable. However, if a bunch of stupid amateurs were intent on getting themselves killed, so be it.

But Chapman had kept the best till last. Would they like to know where they could find Hitler, totally exposed, out in the open, utterly vulnerable? This time there was a distinct reaction.

Chapman had thought it all out. His had been no idle offer to kill Hitler even if it had been dismissed as lacking gravitas by his MI5 controllers. Months before, a visit by Chapman to the local German hospital had coincided with an air raid and, as the sirens had wailed their mournful warning, he had cheerfully assisted in trundling bedridden patients to the underground shelter where he had cowered with the rest. It had been there that he had become acquainted with a wounded American POW airman, asking him how he felt to be on the receiving end of a bombing raid. The reply had surprised and intrigued him. It depended, the airman had said, on which planes were doing the bombing. It seemed that the B17s and the Lancasters gave such a long warning of their approach that the trips to the shelters became no more than irritating inconveniences. But the Mosquito raids, the airman had said, they were quite another matter, so totally without warning, just so long as they bombed on their first approach, that, apart from the damage done, the effect on morale was devastating.

It had been following this chance meeting that Chapman had begun putting two and two together and, at last, the perfect opportunity was presenting itself. His main task now was to convince his controllers and, if they were going to take up his plan, they must hurry. They had less than a week to prepare. First he must overcome the infuriating nonchalance he knew to be no more than a façade. Gradually, he had the satisfaction of seeing their true excitement as he told his tale.

With indecision in the west and impending defeat in the east, the Berghof, while a safe sanctuary, was also becoming to Hitler something of a prison. His bodyguards discouraged even his visits to the nearby Kehlstein, the Eagle's Nest, a fiftieth birthday gift from Martin Bormann, on account of the fact that there were no shelters there. So the proposed presentation of new uniforms and inspection of new equipment, to take place at the Schloss Neuschwanstein, would be a welcome day's diversion.

Postponed several times, the last due to the loss of the equipment in an air raid on a marshalling yard, Hitler was determined not to miss the occasion, overriding all objections from his bodyguards. The fact that it would take a week or 10 days to collect a new display to put before him only served his purpose, a good excuse to delay the evil day when he must leave his beloved Bavaria for the stark reality of Rastenberg. The only thing in doubt, Chapman admitted, was the precise date of the inspection which had yet to be fixed. However, he hastened to add, General Olbricht, who had daily conferences with Hitler, had guaranteed at least 24 hours' notice. Surely, Chapman argued, that would be sufficient if the planes were kept on 24 hour standby at immediate notice?

On being approached, Ludlow-Hewitt, now as devoted to his Mosquitos as Harris had been to his Lancasters, needed no convincing. What was there to lose? He agreed that planes from his two most experienced squadrons, Nos. 105 and 139, must carry out the attack, senior crews from other squadrons, experienced in V1 site raids, to be drafted in if necessary. The crews would not be informed of the true target though they would obviously sense the raid's importance from the degree of "flap" on. Hints at a major Gestapo junket might be dropped. One squadron would appear to be heading for Munich, the other, taking a different route, Regensburg. Timing would be critical.

British castles were built to withstand siege from hostile armies. Built of local stone, making use of cliff, bend in a river or stretch of shoreline in their defences, they tend to blend with the landscape. With vast, unbreachable ramparts, an inner keep was a last resort, the medieval bunker. The German Schloss, in contrast, is usually found on top of a mountain, a pinnacle of wealth and power. Neuschwanstein was a classic example, one of Ludwig II's creations, much loved by Hitler's favourite composer, Wagner. Of white stone, it stood out against the wooded hills around it, visible for all to see. There were no archers' embrasures, only windows from which to look down on the villagers below. There were no ramparts, simply a spacious, sunny courtyard, wide open to the south. Easily identifiable, the soaring spires were no turrets, mere potency symbols.

As Hitler strutted the courtyard, approving this badge, disapproving that belt, congratulating some designer on his new weapon of destruction, he could have had no inkling that he had but moments to live. With virtually no warning, even if there had been somewhere to run, he must have died in the first bomb bursts, long before the remaining Mosquitos reduced an exquisite example of Teutonic beauty to smoking rubble. Olbricht, having observed at a safe distance, raced to confirm Hitler's death before signalling Stauffenberg. Fromm gave the order and Valkyrie was put in motion. Within hours, Beck found himself the new Head of State, accepted as Commander in Chief of the Army. Rommel, now no longer required to struggle with his conscience, could simply obey orders.

The question remained; what would the Allies, particularly the British, do? How would they react? The conspirators had good reason not to trust the British to come to their help. Perhaps, being now under the overall command of an American, things might be different. Germany could fight on on two fronts for another year or so, resulting in an uncontrolled hostile occupation of a devastated homeland, but their High Command now accepted that ultimate military defeat was inevitable. They recognised also that mere withdrawal to pre-war frontiers would never be acceptable to the victors and that they must prepare themselves for foreign occupation of the Fatherland. But by whom: the Russians, Western Allies or both? Stark memories of SS atrocities in the east did not augur well for a Russian occupation by the army of a nation with a death toll running into millions. Occupation by the Western Allies was likely to be altogether a more gentlemanly business. It was true that at Casablanca, it had been agreed that unconditional surrender alone would be accepted but the Russians had needed reassuring that there would be no unilateral peace negotiated. But no one had mentioned unilateral unconditional surrender. If the Germans were prepared to lay down their arms on one front and one front only, there was little the Western Allies could do about it. Surely, that would be a matter purely for the Germans. In the event, there was no need even for this degree of collusion on the part of the Allies. It was in the Germans' interest that the Western Allies did nothing to antagonise the Russians by unilaterally negotiating peace. Sooner or later, the Russian and Allied armies must meet. The last thing the Germans wanted was a new war, fought to the death on German soil, between two vast ideologically incompatible

The Trenchard Touch

armies. Germany had suffered enough. No, the war must appear to go on and, after all, they had in Rommel the past master in the art of fighting withdrawals, skills honed to perfection in the sands of Libya and Tunisia. It would be North Africa all over again, Rommel on one side, Montgomery on the other. Honour, even respect, such as had existed in the desert would be maintained on both sides. As a result, fighting a purely rearguard action, German divisions were released to reinforce the eastern front, keeping Stalin's hordes at bay as the Allies were eased into total occupation of Germany, up to the Polish border where a cold iron curtain fell on an uneasy peace between two implacable political foes. Germany could now begin the long haul to democratic recovery.

All stemming from the enlightened use of one of the war's outstanding aircraft.

Bibliography

Mosquito - The Wooden Wonder
Edward Bishop
Airlife Publishing Ltd 1995

Famous Bombers of the Second World War
William Green
Macdonald and Co (Publishers List)

Halifax
Bruce Robertson
Ian Allan Ltd 1990

The Mosquito Log
Alexander McKee
Souvenir Press Ltd 1988

Road To Victory
Martin Gilbert
Wm Heinemann Ltd 1986
Michelin House
81 Fulham Road
London SW3 6RB

The Avro Lancaster
Francis K. Mason
Aston Publications Limited 1989

Bomber Offensive
Sir Arthur Harris
Greenhill Books 1990

Inside The Third Reich
Albert Speer
Wiedenfeld and Nicolson 1970

Bomber Command Losses 1942
W.R. Chorley
Midlands Counties Publications 1994

Operation Millennium
Eric Taylor
Robert Hale - London 1987

Bombing 1939-1945
Karl Hecks
Robert Hale Limited 1990

Bomber Command
Max Hastings
Michael Joseph Ltd 1979

The Thousand Plan
Ralph Barker
Reprint Society 1966

The Bomber Battle for Berlin
Air Commodore John Searby
Airlife Publishing Ltd 1991

Sky Fever
Sir Geoffrey de Havilland
Airlife 1979

Churchill by his Contemporaries
Edited by Charles Eade
Hutchinson 1953

The Second World War
Winston Churchill
The Reprint Society 1952

Mosquito
Martin Sharp and Michael Bowyer
Faber and Faber 1967

Zeppelin
Manfred Griehl and Joachim Dressel
Arms and Armour Press 1990

The Great War in the Air
John H. Morrow, Jr.
Airlife Publishing Ltd 1993

Decision Over Schweinfurt
Thomas M. Coffey
Robert Hale (London) 1977

The First Great Air War
Richard Townshend Bickers
Hodder and Stoughton 1988

The Berlin Raids
Martin Middlebrook
Penguin Books Ltd 1988

The Battle of Hamburg
Martin Middlebrook
Penguin Books 1980

High Commanders of the Royal Air Force
Air Commodore Henry Probert
HMSO 1991

Winston Churchill As I Knew Him
Violet Bonham Carter
Reprint Society 1966

B17 Fortress at War
Roger A. Freeman
Ian Allan Ltd 1977

Mosquito At War
Chaz Bowyer
Ian Allan Ltd 1973

Combat Aircraft of World War Two
E.C. Weal, J.A. Weal and R.F. Barker
Lionel Leventhal 1977

Despatches on War Operations
Sir Arthur Harris
Frank Cass and Co 1995

De Havilland Aircraft Since 1909
A.J. Jackson
Putnam, London. 1962

Jean Batten: The Garbo of the Skies
Ian Mackersey
Macdonald and Co 1991

The Sound of Wings: The Biography of Amelia Earhart
Mary S. Lovell
Hutchinson 1989

Monoplanes and Biplanes
Grover Cleveland Loening
Munn and Co Inc 1911

The War in the Air, Vol. 2
H.A. Jones
Hamish Hamilton 1969

The War in the Air, Vol. 1
Walter Raleigh
Clarendon Press 1922

The Aeroplanes of the Royal Flying Corps (Military Wing)
J.M. Bruce
Putnam 1982

Trenchard - Man of Vision
Andrew Boyle
Collins 1962

Early Aviation at Farnborough
Percy B. Walker
Macdonald and Co (Publishers) Ltd 1971

Aviation - An Illustrated History
Christopher Chant
Orbis Publishing Limited 1978

Chronology of the Great War
Ministry of Information
Greenhill Books 1988

Famous Fighter Aces
Bryan Philpott
Patrick Stephens Limited 1989

Air of Battle
Wing Commander W.M. Fry
William Kimber, London 1974

Richthofen
Peter Kilduff
Arms and Armour Press 1994

The Drift to War 1922-1939
Richard Lamb
W.H. Allen and Co plc 1989

English History 1914-1945
A.J.P. Taylor
Oxford University Press 1965

To Kill Hitler
Herbert Molloy Mason
Michael Joseph Limited 1979

The Rise and Fall of the Third Reich
William L. Shirer
The Reprint Society (Secker and Warburg Ltd) 1962

Despatch on War Operations
Sir Arthur T. Harris
Frank Cass and Co Ltd

The Allied Bomber War
Maurice Harvey
Spellmount Ltd

Tales From The Bombers
Chaz Bowyer
William Kimber & Co Limited

Wonder Aces of the Air
A.J. Smithers
Gordon and Cremonesi Publishers, 1980

Lancaster at War 2
Mike Garbett and Brian Goulding
Ian Allan Ltd 1979

Lancaster at War 4
Alex Thorne
Ian Allan Ltd 1990

The Mighty Eighth
Roger A. Freeman
Arms and Armour Press 1991

United States Strategic Bombing Survey
European War
September 30, 1945

History at War
Noble Frankland
Giles de la Mare Publishers
3, Queen Square,
London WC1N 3AU

Plotting Hitler's Death
Joachim Fest
Phoenix 1997

World War 1
Susanne Everett
Bison Books Corps
17 Sherwood Place
Greenwich
CT 06830
USA

The Allied Bomber War
Maurice Harvey
Spellmount Ltd 1992
12, Dene Way
Speldhurst
Tunbridge Wells
Kent TN3 0NX

Illustrated History of World War 1 in the Air
Stanley Ulanoff
Arco Publishing Company Inc 1971
219, Park Avenue South
New York
N.Y. 10003

British Aviation, The Pioneer Years, 1903-1914
Harald Penrose
Cassell Ltd 1967
35, Red Lion Square,
London WC1R 4SG

The Guiness Book of Air Facts and Feats
Guinness Superlatives Ltd 1977
2, Cecil Court
London Road
Enfield
Middlesex

Index

accuracy of bombing 120, 125, 146, 149
Admiralty 12, 26, 28, 46, 62, 83, 105
Advisory Committee for Aeronautics 8-9, 18
Aeronautical Inspection Directorate 22
Air Battalion of the Royal Engineers 13
Air Board 40
Air Council 46-7, 93, 96, 104
Air Ministry 52-3, 59, 76, 79-80, 83-4, 93, 109
Airco 22, 25, 26-27, 37, 41, 55
  sold out to BSA 58
Aircraft Factory 11, 13, 19, 21-2, 37, 39, 41, 55
airframe factories bombed 147-8
airships 8, 9-10, 23
Albatross fighters 35
Allied Air Forces 145
Amiens jail 129, 149, 154
Anderson, Sir John 135
Army 8, 13, 18, 20, 102, 113-14, 134
  Bristol fighters 68
  Germany 72-3, 85-6, 94, 106
  India 56
  peacetime 52-4, 56-7
  Portal 145
  Royal Flying Corps 24-5
  separate air force proposed 45, 46, 53, 60, 63
  Somaliland 57
  Trenchard 16-17
  WWI 24-6, 28-30, 39-40, 45, 46
Army Council 46

Army Group Centre 139, 140, 143
Arnold, General (USAAF) 104, 105, 120, 125, 126
Asquith PM, Herbert 8, 13, 18, 39, 42
Attlee, Clement 119
Austria 86
Auxiliary Air Force 68
Avro 23, 55, 81, 92, 97, 104, 109

B17 bombers 84, 125, 127-9, 148, 150, 155
Bailey, Lady 65
Baldwin PM, Stanley 71, 77-8, 136
Balfour, Lord 63
Ball, Albert (pilot) 36
ball bearings 124, 126, 131
balloons 9-10, 13, 15, 21
Baring, Maurice 29-30, 57, 113
Batten, Jean 74, 78
Battle (aeroplane) 95
Battle of Britain 98-9, 103, 132, 147, 152
Battle of Cambrai 46
Battle of Omdurman 14
BE (Bleriot Experimental) aeroplanes 12-13, 20-1, 23, 34, 37, 39
Beatty, First Sea Lord 59, 63, 135
Beaverbrook, Lord 58, 98, 104, 109, 123
Beck, General Ludwig 85, 87, 89-90, 141, 157
Becker, Oberleutnant Martin 132, 152
Bedford, Duchess of 65
Bell, Dr George (Bishop of Chichester) 115, 139

171

Bentley, Flight Lieutenant 64
Berlin bombed
    WWI 27, 44, 54
    WWII 92, 95, 101, 116, 121,
    127-32, 150-1, 152
Beta I 9, 10
Birmingham 106
Bishop, Billy (pilot) 36
Bishop, Ronald (designer) 92, 94
Black, Tom Campbell (pilot) 75
Blenheim bombers 79, 95, 96, 111,
    146
Bleriot, Louis 5, 7, 8, 12, 22, 23
Blumenberg, Werner 88
Boeing 125
Boelke (pilot) 36
Boer War 14, 16-17
Bohm-Tettelbach, Hans 89
bomb loads 36, 43, 79-80, 96-7,
    98, 107
    Lancasters 128, 130, 153
    Mosquitos 118, 125, 128-9, 150
bombers 47-50, 67-9, 71, 78-84,
    98-110, 125-32
    American 125, 126-7, 146-8
    attacking ships 63
    B17s 84, 125, 127-9, 148, 150,
    155
    Comets 75, 76, 83
    converted for civil aviation 65
    German 43-4, 46, 68, 95, 101,
    106-7, 110
    heavy 79-84, 92-3, 95-7, 102-4,
    107-9, 111-12, 118-20, 127-
    32, 146, 152-6
    Mosquitos 98-106, 109, 112-13,
    118-21, 125, 128, 132, 149-
    50, 152-7

peacetime 54-5, 62
    RAF 50, 68, 71, 78-80, 82
    WWI 25, 34, 36-8, 42-4, 46
    WWII 95-7, 98-110, 111-13,
    118-21, 125-32
Bormann, Martin 156
Bottomly, Air Marshal 130
Boyle, Katherine (Lady Trenchard)
    57-8
Brancker, Sir Sefton 32, 37, 64-5
Brequet 5
Bristols 35, 38, 55, 57, 68, 79
British Air Commission 103
Broad, Hubert (pilot) 75
Brownshirts 72-3, 85
BSA 58
Bufton, Air Commodore 124, 125,
    126
Butler, Alan 65, 91, 99

Camm, Sydney 67
Canada 33
Canaris, Admiral Wilhelm 87, 88,
    139, 142
Capper, Colonel J E 9, 10, 11-12
Carnarvon, Lord 7
Casey, Richard 127
Cathcart-Jones (pilot) 75
Central Flying School 13, 18, 19
Chadwick, Roy 81, 92, 97, 104,
    109, 122
Chamberlain, Austen 59-60
Chamberlain, Neville 78, 90, 91,
    95, 98, 137
Chanak Incident 60
Channel Islands 100
Chapman, Eddie 100-1, 116-17,
    143-4, 153-6

Cherwell, Lord (Frederick Lindemann) 77-8, 107, 110, 127
Cheshire, Group Captain Leonard 149
Chichester, Francis 66
Churchill, Winston 13, 19, 122, 124, 132-3, 137
  Baldwin 77-8
  bombers 98, 101-3, 107-9, 153
  bombing policy 45, 112, 115, 127-8, 153
  defence cuts 68
  friend of Trenchard 16, 58, 136, 137
  German attempt to stop Hitler 88
  Iraq 60
  peacetime 52-3, 55-7, 59
  RAF 52-3, 55-7, 59
  WWI 28, 29, 39-41, 44, 45
Civil Flying Regulations 53
Clarkson, Richard 92
Clemenceau, Georges 53
Cobham, Sir Alan (pilot) 58, 64-6
Cody, Colonel 7, 12, 13, 22
Cologne bombed 49, 112
Comets 75, 76, 83
Committee for Imperial Defence (CID) 18, 19, 62
Cooper, Duff 78, 144
Copenhagen bombed 119
Coventry bombed 115
Cresta Run 17, 19
Curzon, Lord 40-1, 42, 57
Curtiss Fairey Foxes 65
Czechoslovakia 86-91

Dakota (DC3) 76
DC2 (aeroplane) 74-5, 76

de Havilland, Geoffrey 1-7, 10-14, 18-22, 55, 58, 122
  Airco 22, 25, 26-7
  bombers 81, 83-4, 97
  civilian aircraft 64-8
  Comets 75-6
  developing new warplanes 91-4, 97
  first flight 1-3, 6
  MacRobertson Race 74-5
  Mosquitos 99-101, 104-5, 149-50
  WWI 23, 25, 26-7, 36-7, 39
de Havilland Junior, Geoffrey 7, 99
de Havilland, Hereward 3
de Havilland, Ivon 3-5
de Havilland, Louie 2, 7
de Havilland Aircraft Company 58, 91-2, 98-9, 116-17
  civilian aircraft 64-6
de la Ferte, Captain Philip Joubert 24, 25
DH (de Havilland) aeroplanes 12, 27, 34, 64-5, 68, 75
  bombers 36-8
DH4 (aeroplane) 42-3, 46, 54-5, 79, 82-3, 92-3
  bombing Cologne 49
  bombing ships 63
DH9 (aeroplane) 55
DH18 (aeroplane) 58
DH88 (aeroplane) *see* Comets
DH98 (aeroplane) *see* Mosquitos
Directorate of Military Aeronautics 22, 46
Directorate of Operations 26
Distant Offensive Patrols 46
Doolittle, James "Jimmy" 127

Douhet, Guilio 69, 147
Dowding, Hugh Caswell Tremenheere "Stuffy" 32, 79, 103
Dragon Rapides 75
Dreadnoughts 8
Dresden bombed 134
Dublin bombed by mistake 107
Dunne 7

Eaker, General Ira 125, 126, 127
Earhart, Amelia 65, 78, 82
Eden, Anthony 139
Edwards, A O 75
Eisenhower, General Dwight D 132, 144-5, 153
Ellington, Edward 71, 78, 80, 82, 136
Ethiopia 77

Fairey Battle 79
Farman, Henri 5, 12, 22
Farman aeroplanes 12, 19, 21-2, 23, 26, 34, 39
Farnborough 9-15, 18-19, 21-2, 23-5, 27, 37, 39
FE (Farman Experimental) aeroplanes 12, 21-2, 34, 39
Feisal, Emir 60
Fellgiebel, General 141
fighters 95-6, 98, 102, 108-9, 111-12, 118, 127, 130, 132-3, 149
  American 146-7
  defence 93
  German 35-6, 101, 147-8
  IAF 48-9
  India 57
  RAF 50, 68, 71, 78-80, 82
  range 127, 146
  rearmament 83
  speed 67, 83, 105, 146
  WWI 27, 34, 35-6, 38
Fisher, Admiral 8
Fleet Air Arm 83, 135, 137
Flying Fortresses 118, 133
Foch, Marshal 52, 62
Fokker aircraft 27, 32, 34, 35, 36
France 48, 52, 62, 92, 137
  bombing 49-50
  Comets 76
  early aeroplanes 5, 7, 10, 11-12, 18, 22
  RFC 41, 47
  WWI 23-6, 29, 31, 35, 36-7, 40-1, 46
Freeman, Wilfrid 24, 36, 37, 79, 92-3, 97, 98-9
  Ministry of Aircraft Production 120, 128
Mosquitos 104, 109, 120
French, Sir John 9, 24
French Air Force 31, 35, 76
Fromm, General Fritz 141-2

Garbett, Dr (Archbishop of York) 115
Gavotti, Lieutenant 20
Germany 62, 74, 152-9
  air force 76-7
  airships 9-10
  Army 72-3, 85-6, 94, 106
  attempt to stop Hitler 87-91, 117, 138-44
  Hitler's rise 72-3, 85-7
  industry bombed 42, 48-9, 54, 147-8

174

invading Channel Islands 100-1
leaves World Diasarmament
 Conference 71
London bombed 8, 9, 28-9, 39,
 43-6, 101, 106-7, 114
rearmament 71-2, 74, 77, 78-9,
 82
WWI 23, 27-35, 39-46, 48-9
WWII 94-6, 98-110, 111-17,
 120-1, 122-32, 134-51
Gipsy Moth (aeroplane) 66
Gloster (jet aeroplane) 118
Gnome (aeroplane) 22
Goebbels, Dr 121, 122, 150
Goerdeler, Carl 89, 138, 141
Goering, Herman 76, 94, 101, 118-19, 121, 137
Goodyear 137
Gordon Bennett Cup Race 12
Gotha bombers 43, 44, 46, 68
G-plan furniture 99
Grahame-White, Claude 6, 7, 12
Green, Major F M 10-11, 13, 22
ground strafing 30, 33
Guest, Major Frederick 59, 61
guns on aeroplanes 20-2, 27, 37, 98, 105

Hagg, Arthur 58, 75, 92
Hague Peace Conference 8
Haig, Douglas 24-6, 30-1, 41, 44, 49, 52, 54, 110
Haldane, Lord 9, 10, 68
Halder, Franz 72, 87, 88, 90, 91
Halford, Frank 58, 75
Halifax, Lord 89
Halifax aeroplanes 80-1, 95, 97, 102-4, 107-8, 111, 129

Nuremberg 132, 152
Hamburg bombed 114-16, 122, 127, 131
Hampdens 79, 95, 96
Handley Page aeroplanes 44, 54, 56, 79, 80
Hankey 136
Harland 80
Harper, Robert 92
Harris, Arthur "Bomber" 57, 110, 111-14, 117-19, 121, 122-33, 152-3, 156
  cooperation with Americans 144-5, 149
  India 68
  RAF expansion 79
Hart, Captain Basil Liddel 115
Hawkers 67, 79
He178 (jet aeroplane) 118-19, 122
Hearle, Frank 6-7, 11, 22, 58
Hearle (nee de Havilland), Ione 22
Hearne, R P 8, 29
Heinz, Captain Friedrich Wilhelm 90
Henderson, Major General David 14-15, 18-22, 23-6, 29, 33-4, 38, 40-1, 44, 46
  formation of air force 46-7, 48, 58-9
Henderson, Sir Nevile 90
Heydrich, Reinhard 122, 139
Hill, A V 110
Himmler, Heinrich 122, 142, 143
Hindenberg, President Paul Ludwig Hans von Beneckendorff und 72-3, 88
Hinkler, Bert 65

175

Hitler, Adolf 72-3, 76-7, 85-7, 94, 102-3, 134, 154-7
German attempt to stop 87-91, 117, 138-44
jet aeroplanes 119
not photographed after bombing 122
Hoare, Sir Samuel 60, 63, 82
Home Army 141-2
Hopner, General 142
Hore-Belisha 82
Houston, Lady 67
Hurricane fighters 98

Immelmann (pilot) 36
Independent Air Force (IAF) 48-50, 52
India 15, 16, 40-1, 56-7, 68, 71
Ingalls, Laura 66
Inskip, Sir Thomas 82
Inter-Allied Independent Air Force 50
Invergordon 135
Iraq 59, 60-1, 68, 71
Ironside, General 90
Italy 142

jet aircraft 118-19
Johnson, Amy 66, 74, 75
Joint War Air Committee 40
JU88 (aeroplane) 99, 106
JZ38 (aeroplane) 28

Keitel, Wilhelm 86
Kessler, Dr Philip 126
King's Cup Race 64
Kitchener, Lord 14, 17, 23-6, 28, 30, 40-1

Kordt, Erich 90
Kordt, Theo 89, 90
Kreisau Circle 138, 142

Ladysmith 9, 14
Lancaster bombers 81, 95, 97, 102-4, 126-31, 155-6
 bomb load 128, 130, 153
 compared with Mosquitos 118-20, 128, 149, 150
 daytime bombing raid 111-12
 equivalent bombers in WWI 43
 Freeman 92, 109
 Nuremberg 132, 152
Langley, Samuel Pierpont 11
Laval, Pierre 77
Law PM, Andrew Bonar 60, 61, 63
 daughter weds Sykes 53, 60
Lee Enfield guns 20
Leipzig bombed 131
LeMay, Colonel Curtis E 146
Lend Lease aircraft 104
Lewis guns 22, 37
Liberators 148
Liberty 12 engines 36
Light Night Striking Force 150, 153
Lightnings 121
Lindbergh, Charles 36, 65
Lindemann, Frederick (later Lord Cherwell) 77-8, 107, 110, 127
Linnarz, Hauptmann 28, 39
Lloyd-George PM, David 41-2, 43, 52-3, 77, 88
 resigns 60-1
 separate air force 46, 47, 48
Lloyd-George, Megan 54
London Aeroplane Club 64, 65, 91
London bombed

WWI 8, 9, 28-9, 39, 43-6
WWII 101, 106-7, 114
Ludlow-Hewitt, Sir Edgar 63, 82, 95, 97, 149-50, 153, 156
Luftwaffe 76-7, 93, 94, 106, 147

Macanese, Major Duncan 19-20
MacArthur, General Douglas 125
MacDonald PM, Ramsey 68, 71, 135
MacRobertson Race 74-5
Mad Mullah of Somaliland 56-7
Mahmud, Sheik 61
Manchester bombers 81, 95, 104
Mannock, Mick (pilot) 36
Maskelyne, Jasper 117
Mason-MacFarlane, Colonel Noel 89
Maxim, Hiram 6
Maxim guns 22
ME109 fighters 109, 147
Merlins 92, 99, 121, 133
Meuse-Argonne campaign 50
Michelin prize 12
Milner, Lord 42, 49, 57
Mitchell, Billy 50, 63
Mitchell, R J (designer) 67, 74, 75-6, 80, 100
Mollison, Jim 74, 75
Montague of Beaulieu, Lord 8
Montgomery, Bernard Law 145, 159
Montrose 23
Moore-Brabazon 7, 12
morale 54, 62, 93, 114, 124, 153, 155
  bomber crews 129
  WWI 31-2, 35, 45

Mosquitos (DH98) 84, 93-4, 98-106, 109, 112-13, 118-21, 125, 127-30, 146, 149-50
  bomb load 118, 125, 128-9, 150
  if used as bombers 155, 156-7
  Light Night Striking Force 153
  Nuremberg 132, 152
  reconnaissance 105, 109, 112-13, 118, 121, 130, 132, 149, 152
Moth 64, 65, 66, 91
Mustang fighters 121, 127, 133, 146, 147

Navy 8, 16, 18-19, 28, 31, 39-40, 102, 113-14, 134
  Fleet Air Arm 83, 135, 137
  minor mutiny 135
  peacetime 53, 56-7, 62
  separate air force 53, 59-60, 62-3
Singapore 136
Neuve Chapelle 27, 29
Newall, Cyril 38, 46, 79, 82, 83, 93, 96
Nigeria 17, 137
Nixon (de Havilland Aircraft Co) 58
Nieuport 5
Nieuport Scout 36
Northcliffe, Lord 8
Nulli Secundus I 9
Nuremberg bombed 131-2, 144, 152

O'Gorman, Mervyn Joseph Pius 10-11, 13-14, 22, 29, 41, 55
oil refineries bombed 148-9

Olbricht, General Friedrich 139, 140, 142, 144, 154, 156-7
One and a Half Strutters 35
Operation Flash 139
Operation Foxley 155
Operation Gomorrah 114
Operation Jericho 129
Operation Noball 129
Operation Turk's Cross 43
Oslo bombed 119
Oster, Hans 72, 86-91, 92, 138-9, 142

parachutes 33-4
Paris 23
Pasha, Kamel 60
Pathfinders 119-20, 121, 129-31, 149, 150
Peel 63
Pemberton-Billing MP, Noel 32, 43
Poland 94
police 135-6
Police College at Hendon 135-6
Portal, Charles 68, 97, 99, 101-3, 108-10, 120, 124-5, 144
   Sweinfurt bombing 130
   Tedder 132, 145, 153
Portugal 76
pusher propellers 2, 12, 22, 27

Ralston, Roy (pilot) 129
Rayleigh, Lord 9, 10, 18
RE8 (aeroplane) 35
reconnaissance 9, 14, 20-1, 97
   Mosquitos 105, 109, 112-13, 118, 121, 130, 132, 149, 152
   WWI 23-4, 27-8, 30, 34, 38
Richter, Karl Richard 105-6

Robert's Bodyguard, Lord 15
Robertson, Sir MacPherson 74
Robertson, Sir William 41-2
Roe, A V 5, 7, 81
Rohm, Ernst 72-3, 85
Rolls, Charles 7, 10
Rolls Royce engines 36
   Merlins 92, 99, 121, 133
Romer, Beppo 138
Rommel, Field Marshal Erwin 140, 142-3, 157, 159
Roosevelt, Colonel Elliot 121, 124
Rothermere, Lord 47-8, 56, 62-3
Rotterdam bombed 137
Royal Aero Club 12
Royal Air Force (RAF) 35, 47-8, 52-63, 64, 67-70, 100-2, 106-7, 116, 137
   bombers 50, 68, 71, 78-80, 82, 95, 125
   compared with civil aviation 67-9
   cooperation with Americans 144-9
   dropping bombs to French Resistance 139
   dropping leaflets 98
   expansion 78-80, 82, 92
   Iraq 60-1
   Ludlow-Hewitt 150
   Singapore 136
   Somaliland 56-7
   Trenchard 53, 55-63, 67-9, 134, 145
Royal Aircraft Establishment 104
Royal Dutch Air Lines 74
Royal Flying Corps 18, 21, 23-35, 39, 41, 46, 58

Military Wing 18, 20, 23-6
Naval Wing 18
Trenchard 25-6, 28-35, 41, 47
Royal Naval Air Service (RNAS) 19, 28, 32, 36, 46, 54
Royal Navy *see* Navy
Rubin, Bernard 75
Russia 142, 143, 158-9

Saarbrücken bombed 38
Salisbury, Marquess of 115
Salisbury Committee on Strategy 63
Salmond, John 48, 52, 54, 56, 68, 71, 135-6
   Iraq 61
Santos-Dumont, Albert 5
Saundby, Robert 113, 125, 132, 152
Saunders, Jason 3, 4, 5-6, 7
Schenk, Klaus Phillip 140
Schnauffer, Heinz Wolfgang 129
Schneider Trophy 67
Scholl, Hans and Sophie 138
Scott, A J (War Reserve Police Constable) 106
Scott, Charles (pilot) 75
Schweinfurt bombed 124-7, 130-2, 146, 149, 152
SE5 (aeroplane) 35-6
Selbourne, Lord 111
September Plot 91, 138
Shorts 19, 55, 80
Simon, Sir John 76
Simpson, Wallis Warfield 77
Sinclair, Sir Archibald 102-3, 110, 115
Singapore 70, 136
Slessor 68, 124

Smith, Charles Kingsford 65
Smith, F E 77
Smolensk 139
Smuts, Jan Christiaan 43-4, 45, 46
Somaliland 56-7, 60, 61
Somme campaign 31, 41-2
Sopwith Camels 35, 38, 55
South Africa 9, 14, 16-17, 25, 42
Southampton docks 52-3
Southern Nigerian Regiment 17
Spaatz, Carl "Tooey" 124, 125
Speer, Albert 122-4, 126-7, 130-1, 141, 147-8
Spitfires 100, 105
Staaken R VIs 43
Stag Lane 58, 64, 66, 91, 94
Stirling bombers 80, 81, 95, 102, 107, 111, 129
Stroelin, Dr Karl 143
Stuttgart bombed 143
Supermarines 76, 80
Swinton, Lord 79
Sykes, Sir Frederick 14-15, 18-22, 23-6, 32, 37-8, 40, 44, 47-9
   Chief of Air Staff 48-9, 53
   Controller General of Civil Aviation 53, 60
   loss of influence 63
Sykes (nee Bonar Law), Isabel 53, 60

Taft, President 12
Tedder, Arthur 68, 79, 132, 144-5, 153
Templer, Colonel James 9
Thomas, George Holt 22, 26-7, 58
Tiger Moth 66, 82
tractor aircraft 21, 27, 36

Trenchard, Hugh Montague "Boom"
  14-17, 19, 23-6, 28-38, 40-2, 44
  AAF 68
  Baring 30
  Berlin 150-1
  bombers 76, 79, 81-4, 93, 96-7,
    110
  bombing policy 30-8, 44-51, 54,
    62, 69-71, 137, 144, 150
  buying American aeroplanes 65
  Chief of Air Staff 47-8, 53, 55-6
  commerce 137
  Commissioner of Metropolitan
    Police 135-6
  compared with Harris 111-14,
    122, 127, 133
  Curzon 41
  Farnborough 23-5
  IAF 48-50
  marriage 57-8
  peacetime 52-6
  RAF 53, 55-63, 67-9, 134, 145
  retirement 70-1, 134-5
  RFC 25-6, 28-35, 41, 47
  Royal Scots Fusiliers 15, 40
  South Africa 16-17, 42
  Southampton docks 52-3

United Africa Company 137
United States 36, 54, 104, 124-7,
  129-30, 133, 158
  Chapman 116-17, 143
  cooperation with RAF 144-9
  Mosquitos 120-1, 129

V1500 bombers 44
Vansittart, Sir Robert Gilbert 89
variable pitch propellers 92

Victoria Cross 21
Vickers 54, 55, 81
  guns 22, 37
Voisin, Charles and Gabriel 5, 12
Voisins 13, 20, 21
von Blomberg, General Werner 85
von Brauchitsch, Walther 90
von Falkenhausen, General
  Alexander 143
von Fritsch, Baron Werner 86, 87
von Hammerstein-Equord, General
  Kurt 72
von Kleist-Schmenzin, Ewald 88-9,
  90
von Kluge, Field Marshal 139, 154
von Manstein 142
von Moltke, Count Helmuth James
  138, 142
von Neurath 86
von Ohain, Hans Joachim Pabst
  118, 122
von Papen 72
von Ribbentrop 86
von Richthofen, Manfred (the Red
  Baron) 33-4, 35
von Runstedt, Field Marshal 142
von Schlabrendorff, Fabian 139,
  140
von Stauffenberg, Claus 140-4,
  153-4, 157
von Stulpnagel, General Karl-
  Heinrich 90, 143
von Tresckow, General Henning
  72, 139, 140
von Uxkull-Gyllenbrand, Countess
  140
von Witzleben, Field Marshal Erwin
  88, 90, 91, 141

Walker, Charles 58, 83-4, 92
Walker, John 99
Waller (pilot) 75
Wallis, Neville Barnes 79, 81
War Office 12-15, 19, 21
  WWI 26, 29, 32, 37, 39-41, 47
Weir, Lord William 42, 44, 47-50,
  52-4, 58, 63, 82
Wellington bombers 79, 95-6, 102,
  111, 146
Wells, H G 8, 29
Westminster, Duke of 13
White Rose 138
Whitleys 79, 80, 81, 95
Whittle, Frank 118

Wilson, President Woodrow 47
Wilson (CIGS) 53, 59, 61
Wolseley car factory 4
Women's Air Derby 66
Women's Dixie Derby 66
Women's Pursuit Handicap 66
Wright, Orville and Wilbur 2, 5, 7,
  11-12

Yemen 68
Ypres 24

Zeppelins 8, 9-10, 28-9, 39-40, 41,
  43